SAINT FRANCIS OF ASSISI

'A really authoritative analysis . . . essential reading'
Colin Morris, TLS

'Le Goff is one of the most distinguished of the French medieval historians of his generation . . . he has exercised immense influence.'
Maurice Keen, New York Review of Books

'The richness, imaginativeness and sheer learning of Le Goff's work . . . demand to be experienced.'
M. T. Clancy, TLS

'Le Goff pushes us beyond pure "science": he stimulates the imagination, enabling us to perceive medieval culture in ways that we had not perceived before.'
Sharon Farmer, American Historical Review

Known for speaking with the birds, for professing poverty, receiving the stigmata and for initiating the Franciscan order, **Francis of Assisi** is one of the most radical and inspiring figures in church history.

In this celebrated biography, now available in English for the first time, the distinguished medieval scholar Jacques Le Goff paints a detailed picture of the life of Francis of Assisi. Locating Francis in the feudal world of the twelfth and thirteenth centuries and exploring the social and political changes taking place at the time, Le Goff assesses the dramatic influence of the saint on the medieval Church and celebrates his role in the spiritual revival of the Catholic Church.

Jacques Le Goff is Director of Studies at the École des Hautes Études en Sciences Sociales in Paris. His books include *The Medieval World* (1997), *History and Memory* (1996), *Medieval Civilization 400–1500* (1990) and *The Medieval Imagination* (1988).

Also available in English by Jacques Le Goff:

Time, Work and Culture in the Middle Ages

The Medieval Imagination

The Medieval World

Medieval Civilization 400–1500

History and Memory

The Birth of Purgatory

Your Money or Your Life

Medieval Callings

Intellectuals in the Middles Ages

SAINT FRANCIS OF ASSISI

Jacques Le Goff

translated by Christine Rhone

Routledge
Taylor & Francis Group

LONDON AND NEW YORK

First published 1999 by Éditions Gallimard as
Saint François d'Assise

First published in English 2004
by Routledge
11 New Fetter Lane, London EC4P 4EE

Simultaneously published in the USA and Canada
by Routledge
29 West 35th Street, New York, NY 10001

Routledge is an imprint of the Taylor & Francis Group

© Éditions Gallimard, Paris, 1999
Translations © 2004, Routledge

Typset in Goudy by BC Typesetting Ltd, Bristol
Printed and bound in Great Britain by
TJ International Ltd, Padstow, Cornwall

*Ouvrage publié avec le concours du Ministère français chargé de la
culture – Centre national du livre*

British Library Cataloguing in Publication Data
A catalogue record for this book is available from the British Library

Library of Congress Cataloging in Publication Data
A catalog record for this title has been requested

ISBN 0–415–28472–4 (hbk)
ISBN 0–415–28473–2 (pbk)

CONTENTS

CONTENTS

PLATES

PREFACE TO THE FRENCH EDITION

For the near half-century that I have been interested in the Middle Ages, I have been fascinated by two different aspects of the character of Saint Francis of Assisi: first, by the historical figure who, at the decisive turn of the twelfth to thirteenth century and the dawn of a modern, dynamic medieval age, exerted a major influence on religion, civilisation and society. A figure half-religious and half-secular, Francis travelled the roads between the newly burgeoning towns and cities or withdrew to solitary retreats in the time of the full flowering of a courtly society that brought in new practices of poverty, humility and preaching. Marginal to the Church without ceding to heresy, revolutionary without being nihilistic, and active in the most effervescent region of Christendom (central Italy, between Rome and the solitude of La Verna), Francis played a major role in the rise of the new Mendicant Orders spreading an apostolic message for the new Christian society. Francis also enriched Christian spirituality with an ecological dimension which made him appear to be the originator of a medieval feeling for nature expressed in religion, literature and art. The paradigm of a new type of saint, so intensely concentrated on and identified with Christ as to be the first person to receive the stigmata, Francis was one of the most impressive characters of medieval history, both in his own time and from our present perspective.

But the man also fascinated me, the facets of his personality coming alive through his writings and his biographers' narratives. Marrying simplicity with influence, humility with power, and an ordinary physique with outstanding charisma, Francis has an appealing authenticity that opens up the possibility of an approach that is both familiar and sufficiently distant. In the desire that tempts any historian – and I am no exception to this – to tell the life of a man (or woman) of the past, to write a biography that strives to reach his (or her) truth, Francis very quickly became the person who, more than any other, filled me with the aspiration to make him the subject of a total history (far removed from traditional anecdotal and superficial biography), historically and humanly exemplary for the past and the present. What kept me from writing this life is that, on the one hand, I was absorbed in historical thinking and works of a more general nature and, on the other, excellent biographies of Francis already existed, works mainly by Italian and French historians.

As I was continuing to imagine and construct *my* Saint Francis, I limited myself to rapid and indirect preliminary work which appeared, moreover, in Italian and French publications that were not widely distributed. Not satisfied with having invested most of my biographical endeavours in *Saint Louis*, a task rendered very different by the nature of the protagonist studied and by the monumental scale of my efforts, and once again kindly encouraged by my friend Pierre Nora, I resolved to publish all the texts that I had written on Saint Francis.

This publication is part of a historical activity whose purpose is to reflect upon and to renew the history of Saint Francis and the image that he bequeaths to us at the turn of the third millennium, firmly established in an authentic historical fabric and far removed from the pseudo-millenarian lucubrations in which Saint Francis has no place. Among these recent studies are the works of Jacques Dalarun and Chiara Frugoni (see the Bibliography), whose general attitudes to Saint Francis are the same as mine although our areas of study are different. I wrote the preface to Chiara Frugoni's *Saint Francis*, which has just appeared in French translation and which emphasises the man and the iconographical documentation. Jacques Dalarun wrote a long introduction and explanation (useful for reading the present book) for the new edition of my main text on Saint Francis, in Italian, by the friars of Edizioni Biblioteca Francescana (Milan, 1998).

Finally, at Prune Berge's kind invitation, I have just recorded a compact disc on Saint Francis of Assisi for Gallimard's new series, 'À voix haute'.

The present volume brings together four studies. The first appeared in English and Italian in the special number of the international review of theology *Concilium*, in 1981, dedicated to Francis of Assisi in the historical context. Its purpose is briefly to define his position 'between the renewal and restraints of feudal society' at the turn of the twelfth to thirteenth century, when the social changes in which Saint Francis played a leading role confronted the traditions from which he did not escape – a man and a saint always torn.

The second, the principal study, is a general introduction to Saint Francis in a chronological (and hence biographical) form that places Francis in his geographical, social, cultural and historical context. It presents, in as clear and simple a manner as possible, the problems of his writings and biographies, which are closely connected with his image and the interpretation of his character, and it discusses the main themes of his concepts and actions. This paper was published in Italian in 1967, in *I protagonisti*, a series of popularised portraits of great historical figures, and has recently been reissued, as I have just mentioned. This is an attempt to approach and introduce the true Saint Francis, or – perhaps better, since my efforts at objective authenticity do not avoid a certain personal interpretation – *my* Saint Francis.

The two other papers develop aspects of Francis and shed light on his influence on thirteenth-century Franciscan society, in which the internal conflicts of the Order, extensions of the different interpretations of the personality and intentions of its founder, allow us to touch upon the contradictions and struggles of the central Middle Ages. Francis and the Franciscan Order have a dramatic history that had a significant impact on their era. I hope to have revealed this drama.

One of the papers, given at a colloquium in Saint-Cloud in 1967 and published in the semi-confidential acts of the colloquium in 1973, is a study of vocabulary ('The Vocabulary of Social Categories in Saint Francis of Assisi and his Thirteenth-Century Biographers'). To rediscover, to make heard, and to elucidate the words of the peoples of the past is one of the primordial tasks of a historian. Francis, who wanted to act upon the society of his time, expressed himself through the spoken or the written word, and his use of words, ideas and feelings is developed in this text that clarifies the instruments that he used to affect and transform that society. It is a language of action.

Finally, I have examined the influence of early Franciscanism on thirteenth-century cultural models (the subject of a conference at Assisi in 1980, papers from which were published in the volume *Studi francescani* in 1981). This is an outline of the whole cultural universe of that epoch, with the influence of Francis and his disciples located within that universe. Inspired by the concern of Francis and of his

Order to achieve a global understanding of society and culture and to act upon that entire terrain, I have attempted a global approach from a social perspective on this history.

And without, I hope, committing any anachronisms, I have tried to make these pages resonate for the present time with an echo of the voice and the actions of Francis and his brothers, as we search for answers at the dawn of the third millennium.

P.S. Isabelle Châtelet has been the ideal reader of the original manuscript of *Saint François d'Assise*, as she was for *Saint Louis*.

CHRONOLOGY

1181 or 1182	Birth at Assisi of Francesco (Giovanni) Bernardone.
1180–1223	Reign of Philippe Auguste in France.
1182	*Perceval* or *Le Comte du Graal* by Chrétien de Troyes.
1183	Treaty of Constance between Frederick Barbarossa and the cities of the Lombard League.
1184	Pierre Valdès, founder of the Waldensians, is condemned by the papacy as a heretic.
1187	Saladin reconquers Jerusalem from the Christians.
1189–91	Third Crusade.
1196	Beginning of the reconstruction of Notre-Dame de Paris in the Gothic style.
1198–1216	Pontificate of Innocent III.
1200	The burghers and the people of Assisi revolt against the nobles: siege of La Rocca and beginning of the struggle against Perugia.
1202	Battle of Ponte San Giovanni. Francis is taken prisoner in Perugia.
	Death of Joachim of Fiore.
	Leonardo Fibonacci of Pisa composes the *Liber abbaci*.
1203–4	The crusaders of the Fourth Crusade take Constantinople.
1204	Francis's illness.
	Unification of Mongolia by Genghis Khan.
1205	Departure of Francis for Apulia. He visits Spoleto and returns to Assisi.
1206	Conversion of Francis: call to the crucifix of San Damiano, meeting with the leper, renunciation of paternal wealth.

	At the Council of Montpellier, Saint Dominic decides to fight the Cathar heresy by example and preaching.
1208–29	Crusade against the Albigensians.
1209	Call of the gospel at the Portiuncula. Bernard of Quintavalle and Peter Catani become Francis's first companions.
1210	Francis goes to Rome with his first twelve disciples and obtains verbal approval from Pope Innocent III for the first Rule of the Friars Minor (lost).
	The masters in Paris are prohibited from teaching Aristotle's metaphysics; the pantheistic university masters, the Amalricians, are condemned as heretics.
1211	At the diet of Nuremberg, Frederick II, king of Sicily, is proclaimed emperor.
1212	Children's Crusade.
	Victory at Las Navas de Tolosa of the Spanish Christians over the Moslems.
	Saint Clare takes the habit at the Portiuncula.
	Francis's ship, sailing to the Holy Land, is blown off course in a storm to the coast of Dalmatia.
1213–17	James I the Conqueror is king of Aragon.
	Count Orlando de Chiusi donates La Verna to Francis.
1214	Departure of Francis for Morocco. Taken ill in Spain, he returns to Italy.
	Battle of Bouvines.
1215	Fourth Lateran Council, at which Francis may have been present.
	Probable preaching to the birds at Bevagna.
	The English monarchy grants the Magna Carta.
1216	Death of Innocent III at Perugia. The new Pope Honorius III probably granted Francis the indulgence of the Portiuncula.
1217	Chapter of the Portiuncula: missionaries sent beyond the frontiers of Italy. At Florence, Cardinal Ugolino persuades Francis, who was on his way to France, to remain in Italy.
1219–20	Francis in the Orient (Egypt, Acre). He probably visits the Holy Places.
1220	In Acre Francis learns of the martyrdom of several of his brothers in Morocco, and the conflicts that have erupted

	within the Order in Italy. He returns to Italy. He turns over leadership of the Order, of which Cardinal Ugolino is named protector by the Roman curia, to Peter Catani.
1221	Death of Peter Catani. Brother Elias becomes the new minister general of the Order. Francis composes a new rule that is approved neither by the Order nor by the pontifical curia (*Regula non bullata*, cited here as I *Regula*). Composition and approval of the Rule of the Third Order.
1222	15 August. Francis preaches in the great square of Bologna.
1223	Francis writes a new Rule, approved by Pope Honorius III (*Regula bullata*, cited here as II *Regula*).
	25 December. Francis celebrates Christmas at Greccio.
1224	On the heights of Mount La Verna, Francis receives the stigmata.
1225	Francis, in poor health, spends two months with Saint Clare in the church of San Damiano, where he composes the 'Canticle of the Creatures', and is treated by the papal doctors at Rieti but to no effect. Brought to Siena, he composes his *Short Testament* there (end 1225 or beginning 1226).
1226	Death of Francis at the Portiuncula.
1228	16 July. Cardinal Ugolino, having become Pope Gregory IX, canonises Francis.
	Vita prima (*The First Life*) of Francis by Thomas of Celano.
1230	25 May. Francis's body is placed in the sumptuous basilica of Assisi, whose construction brother Elias has ordered.
	28 September. In the bull *Quo elongati*, Gregory IX interprets the Rule of Francis in a moderate sense and denies any legal authority to the *Testament* of Francis in the Order of Friars Minor.
1234	Canonisation of Saint Dominic (died in 1221).
1248	*Vita secunda* (*The Second Life*) by Thomas of Celano.
1251	*Tractatus de miraculis Sancti Francisci* by Thomas of Celano.

1260   The general chapter of the Friars Minor at Narbonne commissions Saint Bonaventure, the minister general of the Order, to compose a 'good' biography of Saint Francis to replace all the others.

1263   *Legenda major* (*The Major Legend*) by Saint Bonaventure is approved.

1266   The *Legenda major* by Saint Bonaventure is imposed as the only canonical biography, and the destruction of all previous biographies is ordered.

SELECTED WRITINGS OF SAINT FRANCIS OF ASSISI

Rules, testament and admonitions

Regula non bullata or I *Regula*, 'First Rule'
Regula bullata or II *Regula*, 'Second Rule'
De religiosa habitatione in eremo, 'A Rule for Hermitages'
Verba Admonitionis, 'The Admonitions'
Testamentum, 'The Testament'

Letters

Epistola ad Clericos I, 'First Letter to the Clergy'
Epistola ad Clericos II, 'Second Letter to the Clergy'
Epistola ad Custodes I, 'First Letter to the Custodians'
Epistola ad Custodes II, 'Second Letter to the Custodians'
Epistola ad Fideles I, 'First Letter to the Faithful'
Epistola ad Fideles II, 'Second Letter to the Faithful'
Epistola ad fratrem Leonem, 'A Letter to Brother Leo'
Epistola ad populorum rectores, 'A Letter to Rulers of the Peoples'

Prayers

Canticum fratris solis vel Laudes creaturaram, 'The Canticle of the
  Creatures or Song of Brother Sun'
Laudes Dei altissimi, 'The Praises of God'
Officium Passionis, 'The Office of the Passion'
Salutatio Virginis Mariae, 'A Salutation of the Blessed Virgin Mary'
Salutatio virtutum, 'A Salutation of the Virtues'

Dictated writings

Testamentum Senis factum, 'The Short Testament of Siena'

Selected sources on the life of Saint Francis of Assisi

Vita prima Sancti Francisci, 'The First Life of St Francis' by Thomas of Celano

Vita secunda Sancti Francisci, 'The Second Life of St Francis' by Thomas of Celano

Legenda ad usum chori, 'The Legend for Use in the Choir' by Thomas of Celano

Tractatus de miraculis Sancti Francisci, 'The Treatise on the Miracles of St Francis' by Thomas of Celano

Officium rhythmicum Sancti Francisci, 'The Divine Office of St Francis' by Julian of Speyer

Vita Sancti Francisci, 'The Life of St Francis' by Julian of Speyer

Legenda versificata Sancti Francisci, 'The Versified Life of St Francis' by Henri d'Avranches

Legenda major Sancti Francisci, 'The Major Legend of St Francis' by St Bonaventure

Legenda minor Sancti Francisci, 'The Minor Legend of St Francis' by St Bonaventure

De Vita Sancti Francisci in Legenda aurea, 'The Life of St Francis in The Golden Legend' by Jacobus de Voragine

Legenda Monacensis, 'The Monastic Legend, known as the Legend of Munich'

Sacrum Commercium beati Francisci cum domina Paupertate, 'The Sacred Exchange between Saint Francis and Lady Poverty'

Legenda trium sociorum, 'The Legend of the Three Companions'

Legenda Perusina or *Legenda antiqua Sancti Francisci*, 'The Legend of Perugia'

Speculum perfectionis, 'The Mirror of Perfection'

Actus beati Francisci et sociorum ejus, 'The Deeds of St Francis and His Companions'

I Fioretti di San Francesco, 'The Little Flowers of St Francis'

Lauda O Francesco povero, 'The Praises' by Jacopone di Todi

La Commedia, Paradiso, 'The Divine Comedy, Paradise' by Dante Alighieri

Historia occidentalis, *De ordine et praedicatione Fratrum Minorem*, 'History of the West, On the Order and Preaching of the Friars Minor' by Jacques de Vitry

De Adventu fratrum minorum in Angliam, 'The Chronicle' by Thomas of Eccleston

✠ 1 ✠

FRANCIS OF ASSISI BETWEEN THE RENEWAL AND RESTRAINTS OF FEUDAL SOCIETY

Francis of Assisi was born when the great upsurge of the medieval West was at its height and in a region strongly influenced by this new movement.

For modern historians, the first signs of this development were demographic and economic. From around the year 1000, unevenly in different regions, but steadily and sometimes dramatically – as in north and central Italy – the population increased, in fact doubled. All these people had to be fed, materially and spiritually.

Thus, at first, progress affected the countryside in a society where land was the basis of everything. The changes were above all quantitative and extensive: a great sweep of land clearances opened up new areas for cultivation; open spaces were created or enlarged within the forest mantle of Christendom. Solitude had to be sought further afield. Progress was also qualitative, but this barely influenced the rocky escarpments of Francis's birthplace: in the plains, the wheeled and asymmetrical ploughshare replaced the shallower plough, the new system of yoking made it possible to replace the ox with the more powerful horse, new crops were introduced into the crop rotations that had become triennial, and the advance of cultivated grasslands led to the development of grazing. All this affected mountainous Umbria very little. However, there as elsewhere, the number of mills increased, introducing the first steps of mechanisation in the countryside and the valleys. The increased population began to group together in

This chapter, first published in 1981 in *Concilium: revue internationale de théologie*, in a translation by Paul Burns, has benefited from the corrections and suggestions of Éric Vigne.

villages, built-up areas clustered – and often perched – around the church and castle. This was the process of *incastellamento*, the building of castles and fortifications.

The most spectacular consequence of the demographic and economic upswing was a powerful movement of urbanisation. More decisive than the superficial urbanisation of the Graeco-Roman world, more like the later waves of urban explosion in the nineteenth and then the twentieth centuries, it created a network of towns, which were no longer, as in classical times and the high Middle Ages, military and administrative centres, but were primarily economic, political and cultural ones. To mention only one of the results of this urban phenomenon for religion (that would disappear from Italy in the thirteenth century but continued in a still weakly urbanised England): the figure of the holy bishop holding episcopal power in the old-style towns. From then on, holiness related more directly to towns. The holy burghers, lay people and Mendicant friars accepted towns. The holy hermits rejected them.

Towns became work sites where the division of labour brought a populous and varied artisan class into being, and created – in the three sectors that were advancing towards 'industrialisation' (building, textiles and tanning) – a pre-proletarian workforce which could not defend itself against the subordination of the 'just wage' to the 'fair price' – which is simply the market price determined by supply and demand – or against domination by 'employers'. Towns were places of exchange that attracted or originated fairs and markets sustained by the impetus of trade on both a local and a regional scale. This increased the importance in urban society of the merchants who controlled this trade. Towns were the principal places of economic exchange, which increasingly required a basic means of exchange: money. The merchants in this fragmented Christendom, where there were many different monetary systems, soon produced a new breed of coin specialists: the money changers, who were to become the bankers, taking over this function from the monasteries, which had been credit establishments adequate for the modest needs of the high Middle Ages, and from the Jews, who were confined from then on to the role of consumer lenders (that is, 'usurers'), as were an increasing number of Christian merchants. Centres of the world of money, the towns also became centres of the labour market, where the salaried class steadily grew.

As economic centres, towns also became power centres. Beside and, sometimes, against the traditional powers of the bishop and the lord, who were indeed often the same person, a new group of people, the citizens or burghers, gained 'freedoms', ever greater privileges. Without challenging the economic and political footings of the feudal system, they introduced a variant into it, tending towards liberty ('Stadtluft macht frei', as the Germans say – 'city air makes one free') and equality (the civic or communal oath legally joined equal parties). According to this variant, economic and social inequality was based no longer on birth and family, but on possessions and property, ownership of land and buildings in town, of rents and rates in the form of money.

As in more modern periods of massive urbanisation, medieval towns were full of constant new waves of immigrants. The men and women of the towns were uprooted immigrant peasants.

By the time Francis of Assisi was born, probably in 1181 or 1182, this new society was getting past its phase of anarchical growth, of wild exuberance, and was becoming institutionalised, a process that began sooner in Italy than elsewhere – as much for the corporations of craftsmen and merchants (*arti*) as for the political organisations (*comuni*). To give a single symbolic example, in Perugia, Assisi's great rival in Francis's time, the first known commune building, the Palace of the Consuls (later known as the palace of the Potestat), dates from 1205, when Francis was 23.

But peasant society did not remain static. Even though the *inurbamento*, urban immigration, attracted part of the rural population into the towns, those who stayed in the country successfully demanded new rights from their lords and, in the case of the serfs, liberty. But the reaction of the lords to their financial problems and the growing intrusion of the cities on the *contado*, their rural domains, led to increased economic exploitation for most of the peasant social categories.

In, and faced with, this new society, what became of the Church and the ecclesiastical world? In some ways, the Church was the first to change. What is known as the Gregorian reform, which in time and content spread beyond the pontificate of Gregory VII (1073–85), was more than a process of releasing church society from feudal secular domination. Certainly, the independence of the Holy See from imperial power and the increasing liberty from powerful lay influence in the election of bishops and abbots were significant phenomena. The efforts to eliminate all the economic and social pressures classed as simony were no less important. Above all, the struggle against what Nicolaitanism designated was essential. The struggle against the incontinence of the clergy was not only a moral and spiritual development. By forbidding marriage or cohabitation to the first of the three orders defined at the beginning of the eleventh century by the tripartite schema of the *oratores, bellatores* and *laboratores* – 'those who pray', 'those who fight' and 'those who work' – the Church radically separated the clergy from the laity by imposing a frontier in terms of sexuality.

The Gregorian reform involved an aspiration both to return to sources – *Ecclesiae primitivae forma* – and to achieve the true apostolic life – *Vita vere apostolica*. Faced with the new awareness of the vices pervading Christian society – clergy and laity – it meant a fresh start in the process of Christianisation. It was also, not long after the year 1000, 'the world's new springtime' (in the words of Georges Duby). This inspiration was communicated to all of society through the medium of peace institutions. The Gregorian reform was in a sense the institutionalisation of this inspiration and its absorption into Christian society during the course of the twelfth century.

But the reform of the Church was also a response to the changing world, an effort to adapt to outside events. The response was in the first place institutional. It had three main aspects: the establishment of new religious Orders, the development of the canonical movement, and the acceptance of ecclesiastical diversity.

The new Orders claimed to mark a return to the original Order of Saint Benedict through emphasis on manual labour, which was restored to its place next to the *opus dei*, and on the simple life, expressed as much by the rejection of the traditional forms of monastic wealth as by the plain architectural and artistic style in contrast to the exuberant sculpture, miniatures and precious metalwork of the Romanesque baroque. Of the two most important new Orders, one, the Carthusians, founded by Bruno in 1084, aimed to create the original hermit lifestyle; the other, under Guigues II, prior from 1173 to 1180, proposed an asceticism of four 'spiritual degrees': reading, meditation, prayer and contemplation. The second Order, the Cistercians, founded by Robert de Molesme in 1098 and inspired by Saint Bernard, abbot of Clairvaux from 1115 to 1153, combined economic success with spiritual reform. The Cistercian 'desert' was to be found in the valleys where the Order constructed mills and, making use of mechanisation to free up more time for spiritual life, played a part in technological progress, especially in the field of metallurgy. The Order adapted to the new rural economy, particularly to the development of pasturing and wool production, and popularised a new system: tithe barns, in which the lay brothers live-stock, harvests, work tools and implements were kept.

If the reformed monasticism established a better balance between manual work and prayer, the canonical movement, on its side, created a new balance between the active and the contemplative life, between the *cura animarum* and community life. If the Rules established in 1120 by Norbert de Xanten at Prémontré, near Laon, come within a rural context – calling for poverty, manual labour (the Orders were great land clearers) and preaching – most of the canons of the twelfth century were connected with the urban environment. The adoption of the very flexible and open Rule known as Saint Augustine's – conceived pre-cisely in an urban environment, though an earlier one, very different from that of the twelfth century – allowed the Augustinian canons to combine community life, individual asceticism and parish work.

The *Liber de diversis ordinibus et professionibus quae sunt in Ecclesia* ('Book of the Various Orders and Professions that Exist in the Church'), written between 1125 and 1130, probably by a canon of Liège, which either was left unfinished or has come down to us in an incomplete manuscript, takes note of the large number of statutes for clerics and the religious, and accepts the diversity of ecclesiastical institutions, on the pattern of the divine house in which there are many mansions. It defines these statutes according to their relationship to the world and their relative distance from human habitation: 'Some are completely apart from the masses . . . some are situated near people; others live in the midst of people.'

Lay society was becoming increasingly active in religious life and, although the barriers between clergy and laity were maintained, the latter strengthened their presence in the religious field. Lay brothers played a growing role in the new Orders. The military Orders brought about a certain fusion between the religious and the warrior, the reli-gious life and the code of chivalry. Pietistic groups, beginning in Picardy and Flanders – Beghards and Beguines – then spreading to the foothills of the Alps, were established with the encouragement of clerics such as the Liège priest Lambert le Bègue, who died in 1177, and the famous preacher Jacques de Vitry, who wrote a life of the Beguine recluse Marie d'Oignies before he became bishop of Acre and later cardinal. Towards 1200, the groups of *laici religiosi* and *mulieres religiosae* were fast increasing. Already, the Pataria of Milan and its successors in the twelfth century brought together clergy and laity who were eager for reform.

A council convoked in a field at the gates of Milan in the winter of 1117 by the archbishop and his consuls was attended by 'an enormous crowd of clergy and laity hoping to bury vice and revive virtue'. During the 1140s, the regular canon Arnold of Brescia, who had formerly preached to the people of his native town against the corrupt life of the clergy, roused the Roman laity in a reform movement that was both political and religious.

The Church strove to give fresh doctrinal formulations and religious practices to this new world. The most important developments were undoubtedly those concerning the doctrine of sin and the sacraments.

Theologians, though often in disagreement with each other, like the masters of the episcopal school of Laon, Anselm and Guillaume de Champeaux, and the Parisian Abelard, located the sources of sin in the conscience in a new voluntarist doctrine. Thereafter, intention was the crucial matter. This search for intention nurtured a new practice of penance. The old public confession had gone out of favour and, as far as we can tell, in the hiatus left between the decline of this former practice and the new forms of individual confession, individual or collective penitential practices started to develop. What happened in the twelfth century was that the traditional practices of penance developed into individual confession whispered into the ear of the priest or confessor, although collective forms continued. This development was made a requirement by the canon *Omnis utriusque sexus* of the Fourth Lateran Council (1215) that ordered all the faithful of both genders make at least one individual confession per year. Henceforth, admission of guilt became more important than the penance performed and new terrain was opened up in consciousness: the examination of conscience.

This new form of confession was part of a new concept of the sacraments which were now organised in a septenary in a new system that also included the seven deadly sins and the seven gifts of the Holy Spirit. The changes in ranking inside these sets of seven are worth closer study than they have yet been given. Among the vices *avaritia* – linked to the advance of the money economy – now took first place instead of *superbia*, pride, the supreme vice of feudalism.

A similar development can be noted in the concepts and practices of justice. The main theme here was the search for degrees of punishment proportionate to the seriousness of faults and crimes, considered in relation not only to the scale of facts, but also to the situation and the intentions of the sinners.

Finally, another major innovation was the scholastic revolution. At a certain point urban growth gave a new lease of life to certain episcopal schools, such as those of Laon, Reims, Chartres and Paris. But this renewal proved shortlived, and the monastic schools were also breathing their last. Nevertheless, new urban schools were springing up in a rather disorderly fashion, with two different areas of interest. On the one hand was the draw of theology, which appealed to the intellectual, sociological and political circles flourishing in Paris. The other focus crystallised around law, in the context of the communal expansion in Bologna. Two works destined to become classics were written within a few years of each other. First, in about 1140, Gratian's *Decretum* or *Concordia discordantium canonum*, the first reasoned compilation aiming to harmonise the decretals, basis of the Code of Canon Law that would develop in the fourteenth and fifteenth centuries. Second was the four-volume *Sententiae* by the bishop of Paris (the Italian, Peter Lombard) written between 1155 and 1160. Both works illustrate a new intellectual environment – that of specialists in theological or juridical theory – and a new method (based on rational discussion and argumentation) – that of scholasticism.

In consequence of this great change in the Church a new series of 'ecumenical' councils took place in the West, after centuries without any general council. The four Lateran Councils, of 1123, 1139, 1179 and 1215, were at once the conclusion of the Gregorian reform and the Church's attempt at *aggiornamento*, coming to terms with a century of great change. But their significance was ambiguous, as was the triumph of the papal power whose expression they were. As well as adapting to new ideas, they sought to check and contain – if not completely enclose – the new society. Indeed, despite this attempt at *aggiornamento*, the Church remained subject at the beginning of the thirteenth century to both old and new restraints.

It was particularly slow to take stock of the economic revolution and the growth of urban society, remaining entrenched in rural feudalism. It also made rather rapid strides towards new constraining institutions. The new Orders – the Cistercians, especially – tended towards the acquisition of wealth, exploitation of lay brothers, and stultification in rural life. The arid legalism of a pervasive canon law, as well as the degeneration into bureaucracy and autocracy of the papacy and the Roman curia, began to make themselves felt.

The Church experienced some revealing setbacks: for example, the fruitless Crusade against the Moslems, which was diverted from its original purpose, as is proved by the detour of the Fourth Crusade to Constantinople in 1204, and which was incapable of inspiring the earlier enthusiasm; and (especially) the struggle against heresies inside Christendom itself.

Finally, it was ill adapted, if not powerless, either to suppress or to meet the challenges of history: the onslaught of money, new forms of violence, and Christians' contradictory aspirations to greater enjoyment of worldly goods, on the one hand, and to greater resistance to the increasing pull towards wealth, power and fleshly pleasures on the other.

While scholasticism and the new canon law furnished the Church with the means to theorise about the emerging trends in Christian society, and while works of popularisation – manuals for confessors, model sermons and collections of *exempla* – furnished the unlearned priests with the means to respond in part to the new needs of the faithful, these learned constructs also contributed to widening the cultural gap between the ecclesiastical elite and the mass of the laity, and to stifling, distorting or appropriating the renaissance of folk culture that occurred in the thirteenth century.

Feudalism had become monarchical, and the ruling culture had been influenced by the dominant lay classes, the aristocracy and the knights, whose system of courtly values had been imposed on the new society, even on the urban society of the Italian communes. Francis of Assisi himself experienced the influence of this culture of chivalry and his devotion to poverty had courtly overtones. His chivalrous dream, expressed in his vision of a house full of weapons, never completely faded from his mind. Lady Poverty would indeed be a statement of the rejection of the economic and social values of aristocratic and bourgeois society, but through a courtly and feudal cultural model. In his *De nugis curialum* of 1192–3, the Englishman Walter Map deplored the enticement of the clergy into the whirlwind of princely vices and futilities. Also at the end of the twelfth century, the bishop of Paris, Maurice de Sully, despite his own – and here he was exceptional – modest origins, reminded the peasants in a model sermon – in both

Latin and the vernacular – of their religious duty to pay tithes to the Church and taxes to the lords.

Indeed Gabriel Le Bras had had this to say on the ecclesiastical growth of the twelfth century:

> By a curious chance, the great increase in clerical types was quite unrelated to the needs of the century; it corresponded to the needs of the rich for salvation (or for pomp) and to the comforts (sometimes excessive) of the canons and priests.*

No setback for the Church at the end of the twelfth century is more significant than its failure to cope with the movements of lay people who were either frankly heretical or catalogued as heretical by the Church. The most spectacular and serious movement was undoubtedly Catharism, an actual religion that differed from Christianity and that set up a strict opposition between good and evil, spirit and matter. It affected the lower Rhine basin, certain parts of France and the Empire from the Loire to the Alps, and especially southern France, Provence and northern Italy. It was proof of the failure of the local secular clergy and the Cistercians to whom the papacy had entrusted the regulation of preaching, and also of the Crusade. The consequences were a war waged within Christendom by the Church, the enduring divide between northern and southern France, and the establishment of the Inquisition – one of history's great crimes against humanity.

But even more significant, perhaps, was the Church's incomprehension and fear of the movements of the *laici religiosi*, who did not profess any heretical doctrine. Canon 26 of the Second Lateran Council (1139) had already prohibited the forms of monastic religious life that pious women practised in their homes.

Still more serious were the situation of the Waldensians and the Humiliates. The former developed from the Poor Men of Lyon who had responded to the call of a rich merchant of the town, Valdès, and who, towards 1170, began to dedicate their lives to prayer and good works, reading the Bible, preaching and begging. In about 1175, a group of tradespeople, the Humiliates, formed themselves into a community in Milan for work and prayer, also reading the Bible in the vernacular and preaching. They were soon swarming all over Lombardy.

* Unless otherwise stated, all translations of quoted passages are by Christine Rhone.

Pope Lucius III simultaneously excommunicated the Cathars, Waldensians and Humiliates at Verona in 1184. What did the Church condemn them for? Essentially, for taking over one of the monopolies of the clergy, namely preaching. Walter Map, a church dignitary (an archdeacon at Oxford), was the first to protest: 'Like a pearl cast before swine, shall the Word be given to ignorant people whom we know to be incapable of receiving it, let alone of giving back what they have received?' This usurpation was all the more shocking in his eyes because it was being carried out not only by laymen, but by laywomen.

Certainly, Innocent III made some amends, and from 1196 won back some of the Humiliates, but he changed them by dividing them into three 'Orders'. The first two were groups of genuine religious living according to a Rule; the third comprised what has been called 'a sort of Third Order before its time', whose members practised a trade to cover their own needs and leave something over to give to the poor. Similarly, Innocent III divided the Scriptures into *aperta*, narrative episodes and moral passages accessible to everyone, and *profunda*, statements of dogma which could only be understood and explained by the clergy.

We can thus see what passions, what needs and what demands were at work in certain secular circles around 1200: direct access to Scripture, without the obstacle of Latin and the mediation of the clergy, the right to the ministry of the Word, and the right to practise the evangelical life in the context of the time, the family, working life and lay status. To this we must add the aspiration to equality between the sexes professed at the end of the twelfth century by the Humiliates of Lombardy, the rural penitents of northern Italy, and the Beguines and Beghards of the northern areas of France and the Empire.

Some people, such as the Calabrian abbot Joachim of Fiore, saw the only hope as the coming of a third age on Earth, the age of the Holy Ghost following those of the Father and the Son, brought into existence by a community of 'people of the spirit' – who for that purpose might have recourse to 'active or even revolutionary steps'.

It was in this context that Francis of Assisi reached the age of 20, in 1201 or 1202. His success would issue from the way he responded to the expectations of many of his contemporaries, both in what they accepted and in what they rejected.

Francis was a child of the town, a merchant's son, and his initial terrain of apostleship was urban. But he wanted to bring to the town a feeling for poverty rather than for money and wealth, a sense of peace instead of the internal strife he had known in Assisi, and between Assisi and Perugia.

Giving a new context to the spirit of Saint Martin, who sometimes used to leave his episcopal see in Tours so as to renew his faith in the solitude of the monastery at Marmoutier, Francis sought alternation between work in the towns and the hermit's retreat, moving between an apostolate to all humanity and regeneration in and through solitude. To this society that was settling down and becoming established, he proposed the open road and pilgrimage.

A layman in a time that had seen the canonisation of a lay merchant (Hombon of Cremona) by the new Pope Innocent in 1199, he wanted to show that lay people are worthy and capable of leading a truly apostolic life, like the clergy and with the clergy. Although, for all the pain and strife it inflicted on him, he remained faithful to the Church, out of humility and veneration for the sacraments whose administration required a body of distinctive and respected ministers, he significantly rejected hierarchy and prelacy in his fraternity and as far as possible in his nascent Order. In a world where the nuclear and restricted agnatic family was beginning to appear, but where anti-feminism remained rife and indifference to children was prevalent, he showed, through his close connections with some women, primarily Saint Clare, and through his exaltation of the infant Jesus in the crib at Greccio, his brotherly concern for women and children.

For everyone, free from hierarchies, categories and compartmentalising, he put forth a single model, Christ, and a single imperative, 'Naked, follow the naked Christ.'

In this world that was becoming one of exclusion imposed by the legislation of the councils and the decrees of canon law, exclusion of Jews, lepers, heretics and homosexuals, and where scholasticism (with a few exceptions) exalted an abstract nature the better to ignore the real world, he proclaimed, without the slightest hint of pantheism, the divine presence in all creatures. Between the monastic world bathed in tears and the unconcerned masses sunk in an illusory gaiety, he placed the blissful, laughing face of one who knows that God is joy.

He was the contemporary of the smiling Gothic angels. He was also of his time, both in what he accepted and rejected, and in his doubts and ambiguities.

One major doubt was whether working or begging offered the best ideal of the humble life. How did voluntary poverty relate to enforced poverty? Which of them was 'true' poverty? How should the apostle, the penitent, live in society? What was the value of work?

A basic ambiguity concerned the links between poverty and learning. Is learning not a form of wealth, a source of domination and inequality? Are books not among those temporal goods that we must reject? Faced with the intellectual explosion and the university movement that was soon to take over the Franciscan leaders, Francis hesitated. In more general terms, the question is whether, by the time of his death, Francis thought he had founded the last monastic community or the first modern fraternity.

❖ 2 ❖

IN SEARCH OF THE TRUE SAINT FRANCIS

In quest of the true Saint Francis

On the face of it, nothing could be easier than to introduce Saint Francis of Assisi. He has left us several writings that acquaint us with his perceptions, his intentions and his ideas. As much a friend of simplicity in his writings as he was in his life and his ideals, deliberately ignorant of scholastic subtleties, he did not cloak his thinking and his literary effusions in learned or obscure vocabulary or a style demanding great efforts of elucidation or interpretation. A saint of a new kind, whose sanctity was manifested less by miracles – which were numerous nevertheless – and by the display of virtues – however rare and brilliant – than by the general course of a wholly exemplary life, Francis had in his immediate circle many biographers who not only had documentary information on him but were also concerned with painting him in the truth, simplicity and sincerity that always radiated naturally from him. The friend and brother of all creatures and of all creation, he poured out so much tender care and fraternal understanding to all, so much charity in the highest sense (in other words, so much love) that history has granted him, as though in exchange, the same sympathy and affectionate general admiration. All those who have spoken or written about him – Catholics, Protestants, non-Christians and non-believers – have been touched and often fascinated by his charm.

This chapter was first published in Italian (translated by Lisa Barraffi) under the title 'Francesco d'Assisi' in I protagonisti della storia universale, vol. IV: Cristianesimo e Medioevo, Milan, 1967, pp. 29–56; it was brought out again in 1998 under the title Francesco d'Assisi by Edizioni Biblioteca Francescano, Milan.

Of course his context in geography and history gave him his personal frame and environment, in which his strong attachment to his native place is abundantly clear: to Assisi, located on a network of roads but in touch with the plains and mountains, within reach of humanity but close to solitude; to his Umbria, a land of winding paths on hills and valleys, full of silence and sound, of light and shadow, agricultural and mercantile, vibrant with a simple and thoughtful people, calm and full of burning passion, which sometimes suddenly blazed forth, a people in harmony with the trees, the earth, the stones and sinuous streams, and the company of noble and familiar beasts – sheep, cattle, donkeys and birds – including the doves, crows and jackdaws to which he preached, the falcon, the pheasant, the working bees and the humble cicada that came to sing on his hand; and to Italy, torn between Pope and emperors, cities rising up against one another, nobility and common folk, rural traditions and an advancing economy increasingly dominated by money. And these same ties bound him to his era, that dynamic time of urban development, of anxieties about heresy, of energy ready for death in the Crusade, of courtly poetry, itself split also between brutal passions and refined feelings.

How easy it seems to situate him! And in this amply illuminated setting, the historian is granted, by a final act of grace, another price-less gift: the poetry that issued from Saint Francis and the legend that emanated from him even in his own lifetime are so much part of his character, of his life, and of his action that in him Poetry and Truth become one. More than a century ago, Ernest Renan wondered 'that his marvellous legend could be studied very closely and be confirmed in the main by criticism'.

And yet the simple, open, so-often-told and so-much-depicted Saint Francis is hidden behind one of the thorniest questions of medieval hagiography. Paradoxically, this man who so distrusted book learning and scholarship can only be approached through at least an outline of the reasons that make it so very difficult to use the sources of his story.

Saint Francis in his writings

The first difficulty comes from the writings of Saint Francis himself. First, the saint, in his humility, did not tell his own story. His work cannot therefore be used as a source for any precise information on his life. He only makes allusions to some of the things he did, as examples for his brothers. Thus in his *Testament*, the most 'autobiographical' of his writings, he recalls that he always sought to work with his hands so that the brothers would do likewise: 'And I worked with my hands, because I want to work that way; and I want all the other brothers to work in this honest way of labour.'[1] Furthermore, at least one of his most important writings, the first 'Rule' that he wrote for his brothers in 1209 or 1210, is lost. We know, notably from Francis himself and from Saint Bonaventure, that it was short and simple and essentially composed of a few passages from the Gospels. But the attempts of certain historians to reconstitute it remain very largely guesswork, and it is impossible to rely on this crucial document for a statement as to whether, at that time, Francis had accepted the idea of making himself and his companions into a new 'Order' integrated into the Church or whether he merely contemplated the formation of a little group of laity independent of the church organisation. Also lost, save a discovery made unlikely by the zeal with which researchers with Franciscan leanings have already excavated libraries and archives, are letters (we know of the existence of one to the brothers of France, another to those of Bologna, and several to Cardinal Ugolino, the protector of the Minors and the future Pope Gregory IX), poems, and songs. Of these poems we possess the one was probably the masterpiece, the 'Cantico di frate Sole', 'The Canticle of the Creatures' or 'Song of Brother Sun', but had we conserved the others, some of which we know were in Latin and some in Italian, still others perhaps in French, we would have a more complete picture of Saint Francis the poet – an essential aspect of his personality.

To these losses are added uncertainties about the authenticity of some of the writings that have been bequeathed to us in Saint Francis's name. These doubts relate only to texts generally considered as secondary, but for some of them what is at stake has some significance for an understanding of Saint Francis's thought. Thus, the letter addressed 'to all the potentates, to all the consuls, judges and rectors of the whole world as well as to all others whom this document might reach',[2] and known under the title 'A Letter to Rulers of the Peoples', can be attributed to Saint Francis only because of its contents. No external proof permits confirmation of its authenticity. Now, if the recommendations that it contains correspond to the saint's intentions known from elsewhere, if this call made to the rulers to respect the commandments of God and have them respected by others, seems appropriate to a time when Christendom included temporal and spiritual powers in a single body and appropriate to a man who was always concerned with re-establishing harmony, peace and love in the civil communities and with contributing to the salvation of groups and individuals, it also presents some disconcerting aspects. The insistent allusion to the imminence of the end of the world recalls the apocalyptic ideas of certain Franciscan groups in the thirteenth century rather than the position of Saint Francis himself: he made mention several times of the importance of preparing for the Last Judgment in the life of Christians and clerics but does not seem to have believed in the historical proximity of this event. Similarly, the remarkable act of writing the letter might enshrine a properly 'political' Franciscanism, from which certain contemporary public speakers would willingly draw inspiration, but it seems to go beyond the more discreet and more profound thought and action of Saint Francis.

There is a tendency today to regard the letter to Brother Anthony of Padua as authentic, but its form, at least, remains dubious and the approval that Francis, in contradiction to his usual suspicion of learning, grants in it to the scholastic teaching of theology remains puzzling.

Finally, if the interpretation of the authentic texts of Saint Francis leaves little room for serious divergences, given the simplicity and the clarity of the vocabulary and style of their author, it is not the same for the circumstances of their composition. For example, what role did external pressures play in the changes that the saint made to the Rule of 1221 after it had failed to obtain the approval of the Pope and some of the Minors? Recently – without serious foundation, in my opinion – it has been believed appropriate to attenuate the importance of the *Testament* by claiming that Saint Francis, weakened by illness, dictated this text under the influence of the Friars Minor of the convent of Siena who had received him and that the austerity of this writing reflects the 'extremist' position of these brothers more than that of Saint Francis.

Thus, through this brief sketch of the problems posed by the works of Saint Francis, we can see the main source of the difficulties in Franciscan historiography. During the saint's lifetime, there existed two tendencies in the very heart of the Order, each seeking to pull the founder towards it and to interpret his words and writings in its own way. On the one side were the rigorists who required the Minors to practise total poverty, both collective and individual, to refuse all display in the churches, convents, and liturgy of the offices of the Order, and to keep their distance from the Roman curia, who were suspected of compromising too easily with the times. On the other side were the moderates, convinced of the need to adapt the ideal of poverty to the development of a growing Order of friars, not to dishearten by refusing all exterior comforts the ever greater crowds that were turning to the Minors, and to consider the Holy See as the authentic source of truth and authority in a Church of which the Order was an integral part. Where was the real Francis placed between these two tendencies?

The problem of the biographies

It should be possible to answer this question by studying his life as well as reading his works. However, there is a major difficulty. As a result of the dissent inside the Order of Minors in the thirteenth century, there are no wholly reliable sources on the life of the Order's founder. These disagreements among the Friars Minor began during Saint Francis's lifetime; it was because of them that he returned from the Holy Land in 1220 and composed in 1221 a new Rule that he immediately had to modify; it was because of them that he gave up the leadership of the Order, handing it over as early as 1220 to Peter Catani, and then (after the death of the latter, in 1221) to Brother Elias. These divisions were aggravated after Francis's death, all the more so as Brother Elias, who ruled the Order until 1239 – although he had ceded the ministry general to Giovanni Parenti from 1227 to 1232 – engaged it decisively on the path of pomp, symbolised by the construction of the sumptuous basilica of San Francesco in Assisi, to the exasperation of the champions of austerity. In the second half of the century, the conflicts were accentuated – despite pontifical interventions and, sometimes, because of them – and the two tendencies represented actual enemy factions. The Conventuali (Conventuals) agreed to follow the Rule interpreted and completed by papal bulls that weakened the practice of poverty, while their adversaries – generally called the Spirituali (Spirituals), especially in Provence, or *Fraticelli*, principally in Italy – increasingly swayed by the millenarian ideas of Gioacchino da Fiore (Joachim of Fiore), and increasingly extremist in their austerity and hostility to Rome, found themselves reduced to heretical positions. The great hope that was sparked in them by the election to the papal throne, in 1294, of the hermit Pietro di Morrone was very quickly extinguished, because after six months Celestine V was constrained, in the words of Dante, to make the *gran rifiuto*, to renounce the tiara. Although some Spirituals survived until the end of the fifteenth century (irreducible *fraticelli* or rigorist Minors who became 'Observants'), the quarrel among the Franciscans can be regarded as settled by Pope John XXII in 1322 with the bull *Cum inter nonnullos*, which favoured the side most opposed to absolute poverty and the Spiritual tendencies.

As regards the sources of the history of Saint Francis of Assisi, how-ever, the decisive episode of this struggle took place in 1260–66. In the Order, there were always partisans of the happy medium, wishing to create a compromise between the two extreme factions. Like Dante, they thought of Saint Francis's family:

> His family, whose feet were following
> straight forward in his footsteps, is so turned round
> that the tail has twisted to the head,
> and soon we shall see the harvest
> of the bad tillage, when the tares
> shall wail they are excluded from the bins.
> I do admit that if one searched, leaf by leaf,
> our volume, one could still find a page
> which reads, 'I am what I always was',
> but it is not from Casale or Acquasparta
> that come such readers to the Rule,
> some who evade it, and others who narrow it.[3]

The specific person in whose mouth Dante put these words is Saint Bonaventure who was appointed to the ministry general in 1257 by the moderates to re-establish the unity of the Order, and who adopted a measure fraught with consequences for the historiography of Saint Francis. The Franciscans of the two tendencies had produced numerous biographies of the saint, lending him words and attitudes agreeing with their own position. People no longer knew which Saint Francis to devote themselves to. The general chapter of 1260 entrusted Saint Bonaventure with the task of writing the *official* life of Saint Francis that the Order would from then on consider the only one to depict the true Francis. This life, or *Legenda* (called the *Legenda major* to dis-tinguish it from the *Legenda minor*, an abridged version in the form of liturgical lessons composed by Bonaventure to be used by the choir), was approved by the general chapter of 1263, and that of 1266 took the decision to forbid the brothers ever to read any other life of Saint Francis and ordered them to destroy all the other, earlier writings about him. This was a surprising decision, dictated no doubt by the desire to put an end to internal divisions, and facilitated by the insensitivity of the age to scientific objectivity. It demonstrated a scorn for authenticity that is all the more curious as Saint Francis had, on the contrary, proclaimed his respect for the words and the spirit of authentic texts. Thus in his *Testament* he had declared: 'The minister general, the other ministers and the custodians, through obedience, must add or subtract nothing to these words. Let them always have this text attached to the Rule. When they read the Rule they will also read these words.'[4]

It is true that, as early as 1230, Pope Gregory IX, in the bull *Quo elongati*, had allowed the Friars Minor to disregard this passage from the *Testament* of Saint Francis. If one could neglect the words of the saint, all the more reason to ignore those of his biographers.

Unfortunately for historians, the Franciscans obeyed the order of 1266 so literally that searches for intact manuscripts have proved disappointing. But here we can still hope for further discoveries. Since the publication by the Bollandists, in 1768, of the *Legenda* known as *The Legend of The Three Companions* and of Thomas of Celano's first biography (*Vita prima*), a series of manuscripts have been discovered that limit – in part – the catastrophic consequences of the auto-da-fé of 1266.

It is also unfortunate that Saint Bonaventure's *Legenda* is relatively useless as a source for the life of Saint Francis; anyway, it has to be checked against documents that are more reliable. Indeed, engaged in his role of peacemaker, Saint Bonaventure, while inspired by profound veneration for Saint Francis and drawing on authentic earlier sources, produced a work that ignores the requirements of modern historical science, for it is tendentious and fanciful: fanciful in that it combines sometimes contradictory elements taken uncritically from different sources; tendentious in that it remains silent on anything that would have shown that the Franciscan Order had deviated from certain intentions of Saint Francis and sometimes on essential points, such as knowledge and education, manual labour, the visiting of lepers, and the poverty of churches and convents. Indeed, this Saint Francis of the happy medium is closer to that of the Conventuals than that of the Spirituals.

Until the end of the nineteenth century, it was nevertheless Saint Bonaventure's edited, mangled and saccharine Saint Francis, made even duller by recourse to a mediocre work of devotion written by Bartholomew of Pisa in the first half of the fourteenth century and approved by the general chapter of 1399, that was considered the true Francis.

The requirements of modern historical criticism led, at the end of the nineteenth century, to a revision of the traditional Saint Francis. A foretaste of this revision came with the celebration of the seventh centenary of the birth of Saint Francis in 1882 and the appearance, on that occasion, of Leo XIII's encyclical *Auspicato concessum*. But the real starting point of the quest for the true Saint Francis dates from the fundamental work of 1894 by the Protestant Paul Sabatier.

Since then, Franciscan historiography has developed and also become so complex that only a very simplified summary can be given here.

The essential sources of the life of Saint Francis are considered as ordered around two people, one of them representing the moderate and the other the rigorist Franciscan groups. Because it has been easier to discover more manuscripts of the moderate tendencies, the main issue is the critique of the sources of the so-called 'Spiritual' tendencies.

However, the works of the first group are not as straightforward to interpret as is believed. They are all authored by the Franciscan Thomas of Celano, who composed them at the request of high ecclesiastical personalities. Reputed for the elegance of his style, he first wrote a life of Saint Francis at the request of Gregory IX, the *Vita prima*, completed in 1228. This life, which was very well informed, remains silent on any hint of dissent either within the Order or between the Order and the Roman curia, emphasises the prominent role of Brother Elias, who was then very powerful, and draws inspiration from traditional hagiographical models, such as the life of Saint Martin of Tours by Sulpicius Severus and the life of Saint Benedict by Gregory the Great. Towards 1230, Thomas of Celano composed the *Legenda chori*, a synopsis of the *Vita prima* to be read at matins.

In 1244, the minister general Crescentius of Jesi asked Thomas of Celano to write a new life that would augment the *Vita prima* by bringing in new elements requested by brothers who had not known Saint Francis. He asked anyone who could to help Thomas of Celano by writing their memories of Saint Francis for his information. Thus, the *Vita secunda* presents the following major problems: What are its relationship with and its differences from the *Vita prima*? To what extent does it convey the contributions of those who wrote down their memories to provide documentation for Thomas of Celano? To what degree does the *Vita secunda* suffer from the embellishment of these memories?

Among the sources used by Thomas of Celano were three brothers who had known Francis particularly well – Brothers Ruffino, Angelo and Leo. Brother Leo was in fact the central character in the rigorist group of Saint Francis's biographers. Moreover, this collaboration, which is difficult to define exactly, thus further complicates the problem of the *Vita secunda*.

In the covering letter written to Thomas of Celano in 1246 and sent with their *Legenda*, the three companions declared, 'Rather than report miracles that, in truth, do not constitute holiness but only demonstrate it, we have preferred to communicate the instructive life and the true intentions of our blessed Father.' This new 'progressive' concept of holiness did not satisfy the needs of the crowds, who were accustomed to being sated with miracles. It was to respond to these traditional needs that Thomas of Celano, at the request of the new minister general John of Parma, had to write *The Treatise on the Miracles of Saint Francis* in 1253. Even though these miracles were mainly worked by the saint after his death and the *Treatise* was thus a complement to the two *Vitae*, it nonetheless marks a step backward in relation to the spiritual biography of Saint Francis.

In contrast to this coherent series, well established and exactly dated, of the writings of Thomas of Celano, the opposing group of Francis's biographies shows many gaps and great uncertainties. The central character, as either informer or author, is Brother Leo, who was Saint Francis's confessor and thus well placed to know the saint's inner life. However, none of the works that criticism attributes to him can be definitively classed as authentic. *The Legend of the Three Companions* (*Legenda trium sociorum*) that we possess is probably not the original addressed to Thomas of Celano. It is probably a compilation from the beginning of the fourteenth century, drawing simultaneously on Thomas's *Vita secunda*, on sources authentically attributable to Brother Leo but not used by Thomas, perhaps including his original text, the

Speculum perfectionis (*The Mirror of Perfection*), which may not be an authentic work by Brother Leo either, but was probably composed after his death on the basis of directly transcribed stories or writing by Leo. The *Manuscrit Philippe* is an older version of the *Actus beati Francisci et sociorum ejus* – *The Deeds of Saint Francis and his Companions* – a fourteenth-century compilation close to the *Fioretti*. This manuscript probably includes paragraphs reproducing an original text by Brother Leo. Finally, the most valuable of these texts is perhaps the *Legenda antiqua*, published in 1926, which seems the most authentic of the texts attributed to Brother Leo, but which presents problems as yet unresolved.

Thus, the use of this group of texts comes up against many difficulties. If it seems to introduce a Saint Francis who is more uncompromising, less slick, and more real than the 'official' Saint Francis, let us not forget that it probably also distorts Saint Francis but in the opposite sense. And historians who would like to counterbalance the 'revised and edited' version of Saint Francis with that of Brother Leo are forced to recognise that the auto-da-fé of 1266 succeeded in depriving us of texts that could have been used in complete security.

Among the other texts providing biographical data on Saint Francis, a place apart must be reserved for two works that are more legendary than historical, but that played a primary role in Franciscan mythology.

The first is the 'Sacrum Commercium beati Francesci cum domina Paupertate' ('The Sacred Exchange between Saint Francis and Lady Poverty'), a short epic composed as early as 1227, expressing a theme doubtless born during the actual lifetime of the saint and destined for great success.

The second is the *Fioretti*, a compilation in Italian, assembling, about a century after the death of Saint Francis, brief instructive stories, some of them translated from various small devotional works in Latin, others illustrating through anecdotal examples the maxims of the *Speculum perfectionis*. This very popular work, after nearly falling into discredit due to modern criticism, is now enjoying a revival of some degree. It seems closer to authentic sources than had been believed, is strongly marked by the influence of the Spirituals and re-establishes a certain balance from the favouring of the official Saint Francis. It shows, finally, that very early on Saint Francis had inspired a literature in which legend and history, reality and fiction, poetry and truth were closely blended.[5]

Life of Saint Francis

Francesco Bernardone was born, in 1181 or 1182, in Assisi. His father, a cloth merchant whose business involved travel to France, was away at the time. In his absence, his mother had the child baptised 'John Baptist', after the saint of the desert and of preaching, the herald of Christ, to whom Francis always had a particular devotion. Nobody knows when and how the forename Francis, at that time 'odd and unusual', replaced that of John. Three main hypotheses have been advanced: back from France, the father changed the forename of the infant to that of the country he had just come from; his name was changed as a mark of respect to his mother who may have been French (though there is no proof of this); or a nickname may have been given him in his youth because of his taste for the French language and it lasted on. Of these, the last appears the most credible. The French that he learned before his conversion, because it was the language par excellence of poetry and chivalrous sentiment, continued to be the language of his intimate outpourings. 'When he was full of the ardour of the Holy Spirit,' said Thomas of Celano, 'he spoke out loud in French.' He sang in the woods in French, and one day he begged in French for oil for the lamp of San Damiano that he was repairing. The French language filled him with rapture and jubilation. In 1217, he wanted to go as a missionary to this land of France that he sensed would be receptive to his preaching and whose devotion to the Eucharist he admired so much that he wanted to die there because of this veneration for the Holy Sacrament. In any case, it is not immaterial to note that in a time when names had profound significance and were heavily laden with symbolic meaning, the mere fact of accepting and commonly using an unusual first name demonstrated Francis's will to innovate in his apostleship.

But the young Francesco Bernardone gave no inkling of his future vocation. Thomas of Celano accused his parents of having raised him deplorably and has blackened the depiction of his depraved adolescence, a commonplace of hagiography. But the young man spent his time on the usual entertainments of his social class, no more: on games, idleness, chatter, songs and the latest fashions in clothes. He may have tried to eclipse his companions and become the leader of what has been called, with much exaggeration, 'the golden youth of Assisi'. What is most interesting is that this merchant's son, by a natural reaction of the young generation of his social group, sought to lead a chivalrous lifestyle, to imitate the behaviour of the nobles more than to practise the virtues and the failings of the mercantile bourgeoisie. If he was, indeed, 'a skilled businessman', he was above all 'a big wastrel'. It was his largess that made him comparable to the nobles. Thomas of Celano, who calls him 'very rich', recognises furthermore that the fortune available to him through his father was less than that of most of the young nobles: 'poorer in possessions, he was more giving in his largess'. Another similarity was his culture: a great admirer of courtly poetry, he stood out from his companions as a minstrel, a *jongleur*. A final point was his way of life: he was attracted to war and the profession of arms. Here he was not short of opportunities. In Assisi itself, two struggles were taking place: first between the partisans of the Pope and those of the Emperor, both groups equally anxious to predominate in this well-situated stronghold with its redoubtable fortress of La Rocca; and second between the nobility and the people of Assisi, that is, the old feudal families and the new mercantile bourgeoisie, who, with the support of the common people, formed a *comune* that assured the city its independence of foreigners – Germans or pontifical – and of the feudal aristocracy. This 'popular' party seems to have prevailed. In 1200, the people of Assisi threw the German garrison out of La Rocca, refused to hand over the fortress to the delegates of the Pope and, to strengthen their position further, destroyed it, demolished or burned the palaces of the nobles inside the city and their castles in the surrounding areas, killed off some of them and forced the others into exile, and finally protected themselves by sealing off the city with hastily constructed ramparts. That Francis Bernardone took part in these battles is more than likely. It has even been suggested that working on the construction of the ramparts introduced him to the art of masonry that he practised later as a builder and rebuilder of chapels and churches, starting with San Damiano.

What is certain is that one episode of these struggles ended badly for Francesco Bernardone. The noble families driven from Assisi – like that of the future Saint Clare, the Offreduccio di Favarone family – took refuge in Assisi's old rival, Perugia. To reinstate these families in their personal property and social position, the Perugians declared war on the people of Assisi. Francis took part in the battle between the two cities in 1202 at the Ponte San Giovanni on the Tiber. He was captured there by the Perugians and remained in prison in Perugia for over a year. A characteristic detail reads, 'Since he lived in the manner of the nobles, he was imprisoned with the knights.' Freed in November 1203, he was not diverted from the desire for military glory either by this distressing experience or by a long illness that immobilised him for much of the year 1204. In 1205, he decided to travel to Apulia with a nobleman of Assisi who would serve in the papal armies against the imperial troops. A dream seemed to confirm him in his intention. He saw his whole house full of military dress and weapons. This was the dream of a noble, not of a merchant, as Thomas of Celano noted somewhat maliciously: 'He was not used to seeing such things in his house, but rather piles of cloth for sale.' He interpreted this vision as foretelling his future successes as a warrior in Apulia. He did not yet understand that the vision was symbolic, that he would be called to other battles, to use other arms, spiritual ones. It was indeed on the way to Apulia, in Spoleto, when he was stopped by another vision. He was not to reach Apulia; he was not to be a glorious warrior. His conversion was under way. He was to be one of the greatest saints in the history of Christianity. However, to his new life he would bring the passions of his youth: poetry and the taste for joy that from being profane would become mystical; the generosity that would consist in pouring out not money but words, physical and moral fortitude, all of himself unreservedly; the militant ardour that would enable him to endure every trial and to initiate the assault on all the fortresses standing in the way of his brothers' salvation, the assault of Rome, of the Sultan, and of sin in all its forms.

The conversion

Thomas of Celano's presentation of the conversion of Saint Francis shows inconsistencies, notably due to the difference in tone between the *Vita prima* and the *Vita secunda*. Attempts have been made to resolve these difficulties by assuming that Thomas had disparate sources available to him that he tried to harmonise without great success and by interpreting the two texts on different, but not contradictory, levels. The conversion would be presented in the *Vita prima* in a 'spiritual perspective', or a psychological one, and in the *Vita secunda* from a 'religious' or mystical point of view. Here it is enough to recognise that a conversion is difficult to analyse and that the most important task for the historian is to focus on the themes, on the episodes that marked its stages, and to extract their historical significance. It is note-worthy that, despite the character of sudden illumination, of instant transformation that a conversion always takes on in a hagiography, that of Saint Francis, according to Thomas, extended over four or five years and followed a progressive development in several stages. First, the initial upheaval took place during an illness. Of the nature of this illness that lasted for months, we know nothing, but, from this point on an essential feature in the physical and spiritual personality of Francis is established: he was a sick man. He would suffer until his death from two kinds of illness: eye troubles, on the one hand, and dis-orders of the digestive system, stomach, spleen and liver, on the other. Travels, preaching, fatigue and ascetic practices would aggravate this ill-health. But Francis did not try systematically to mortify his body. His attitude towards it was ambiguous or, perhaps better, ambivalent. The body is the source and the instrument of sin. In this respect, it is therefore the very enemy of humanity: 'Many, when they sin or are wronged, often see it as the fault of their enemy or their neighbour. But that is a mistake, because everyone can master the enemy, that is, the body, which is the instrument of sin.'[6] But it is also the material image of God and more especially of Christ: 'Consider, o people, in what excellent state the Lord has put you, since he created and formed you *in the image* of his beloved son in the body, and *in His own likeness* in the spirit.'[7]

Thus, it is necessary to mortify the body, but in order to put it, like the soul, in the service of God's love. The body is, definitely, like all created beings, 'brother body', and 'our sisters, the illnesses' are vital opportunities for salvation. But we must not give way to them to the point of becoming their slaves if they make the body unfit for the work of salvation and love. Certainly, Francis had no special fondness for doctors, preferring the only real doctor, Christ, but when his eye ailment had almost blinded him, he willingly and humbly gave in to Brother Elias who persuaded him to consult the Pope's doctors by quot-ing to him the words of Ecclesiasticus 38:4, 'The Lord created medicines out of the earth, and the sensible will not despise them.' Similarly, during his stay with the papal doctors at Rieti, he asked one of his com-panions: 'I would like, brother, that you secretly take a zither into hiding and play some decent music on it so as to distract a little my brother the body which is full of pain.' To the brother, who feared what people would say, Francis said, 'Well, let's not talk about it any more! We must know how to renounce so as not to scandalise.' But during the night, an angel would come with a zither to replace the overly timorous brother at the bedside of the sick man.

With roots in the physical pain that began to make him think about human destiny, and established the theme (fundamental in Francis) of the relationship between the *inner person* and the *outer person*, his conversion was revealed first by the renunciation of money and of material goods.

The chronology of the episodes of this stage is particularly confused in the writings of Thomas of Celano.

A first act seems to have taken place when he failed to depart for the war in Apulia. Francis met a poor knight in rags and gave him his coat. Of course, true or false, the gesture tends to make of Francis a new Saint Martin. And Thomas of Celano, who does not fail to establish the comparison, emphasises that it favours Francis, who gave his whole mantle, while Martin gave only half of his.

This was a significant difference between two different personalities, perhaps – Saint Francis was, from the beginning, a man who gave totally – and between two dissimilar times, very surely. At the turn of the fourth to fifth century, the immediate need of Western society was for goods to be shared, redistributed between the old rich and the new poor, while at the turn of the twelfth to thirteenth century, the question was whether or not to possess what money could buy with ever greater ease as the money economy spread.

After this first renunciation, this first symbolic rejection, back in Assisi Francis was chosen by his companions as the chief or king of youth, according to an old folkloric rite. But this profane king gradually withdrew from his subjects so as to prepare himself for a new life by going to meditate in a remote cave, accompanied by a single friend, the intimate confidant of his thoughts. To this friend he revealed the nature of the hidden treasure he said he was seeking and the betrothed that the people of Assisi suspected him of getting ready to marry. The treasure would be divine wisdom, and the spouse the religious life. Thus was prefigured the theme of marriage with poverty.

Poverty was the Lady to whom he was slowly moving closer. Little credence can be given to Thomas of Celano's story that has him go to Rome where he mingled with the crowd of beggars before the basilica of Saint Peter. Indignant to see the meagre offerings made to the head of the Church, the story continues, he gave him everything he had with him. But this call to enrich Rome does not sound like Francis, and it must be seen as one of those pro-Roman episodes introduced by Thomas of Celano and the moderate Franciscans who fabricated them out of nothing.

Events then gathered pace. Shocked by the dilapided state of the little church of San Damiano, which the poor priest who served there did not have the means to repair, Francis gathered a bundle of cloth from his father's house, packed it onto a horse, and went to sell both it and the horse at Foligno. He came back to Assisi on foot and gave the entire proceedings of the sale to the poor priest. Furious at the disappearance of his merchandise, his father had him searched for. Francis hid in the cellar of an abandoned house, where his loyal friend secretly brought him food. Then, having decided to live up to his responsibilities, he left his hiding place and revealed himself to his fellow citizens. Now thin for lack of food, he accused himself publicly of laziness and idleness. This turnaround astonished the people of Assisi, who mocked him, called him a lunatic, and threw mud and stones at him in a foretaste of his persecution and quest for martyrdom, a sketch of the imitation of the suffering Christ, of the Ecce homo. Having heard the uproar, his father came running out, seized him and had him thrown in chains into a dungeon in his house. A few days later, overcome by compassion, his mother set him free. He went to take refuge with the bishop, and there, in the presence of the bishop as official witness and protector, openly facing his father who was livid with rage, he accomplished the solemn act that marked his break with his earlier life and that liberated him. He renounced all his possessions, then undressed completely and, naked, demonstrated that he had shed his past.

In the course of this period, he nonetheless had some doubts. Several times in a dream he saw a hideous deformed woman, exaggeratedly humpbacked. Was this a caricature of the expected spouse? Was it a repugnant image of the miserable life that awaited him? Francis finally cast out the apparition whom Thomas of Celano saw as the Devil and the historian perceives as like the temptation of Saint Anthony – another paradigm of Francis.

He had broken with mundane life; he had not yet become engaged in the new life. Some of his first tentative steps were false steps, showing his uncertainties, his difficulty in sounding the right note, in moving from one life to the other. In a forest one day, when he was singing the praises of God in French, a band of brigands pounced on him, 'Who are you?' 'I am the herald of the great King.' They beat him black and blue and threw him in a ditch full of snow. 'Go then, peasant, you who think you're God's herald.'

Thus, there were still obstacles to overcome. A little later, another great step was made, the only one that Francis mentioned at the beginning of his *Testament* when he spoke of his conversion.

> The Lord gave me, Brother Francis, the grace to begin to repent; when I was still in sin, it seemed to me too painful to visit the lepers, but the Lord himself led me among them and I dealt with them with compassion; and when I left them, what had seemed unbearable was quickly changed into a sweetness of soul and of heart. Then I waited a little, and then I left the world.[8]

The leper's kiss introduced new themes into his life: repugnance overcome, charity to the suffering and to brother body, and service to the most unfortunate, the most insignificant.

What happened next? He used to question God in the church of San Damiano. And, one day, God answered him. The crucifix spoke to him, the crucifix in the painting which expresses a new devotion to the suffering Christ and which still survives today at Santa Chiara. God said to Francis, 'Francis, go and repair my house that, as you can see, is falling all to ruin.' And Francis, who was not yet used to understanding the symbolic sense of the divine word, took the words of the crucifix literally. What were falling in ruins, in fact, were the material houses of God, the churches in disrepair and, to start with, San Damiano. Prefiguring the spiritual reconstruction of the Church, of which he would be one of the greatest artisans, Francis took up a trowel, climbed up the scaffolding and made himself a mason. Another theme entered his life – manual labour. When San Damiano had been reconstructed, Francis worked on the church of Saint Peter near the ramparts, and finally at the Portiuncula, an oratory lost in the forest but close to the two leper-houses of Santa Maddalena and San Salvatore.

The Portiuncula was, in the words of Saint Bonaventure, 'the place that Francis loved most in the world'. It was there that the final act of his conversion took place. God spoke to Francis again, this time, through the voice of a priest who, one day at Mass in the humble oratory of the Portiuncula, read a Gospel text that Francis felt he was hearing for the first time. It was chapter 10 of Matthew:

> Go, said the Saviour, and proclaim everywhere that the king-dom of Heaven is upon you. You received without cost; give without charge. Take no gold, silver, or copper in your belts, no pack for the road, no second coat, no sandals, no stick, for the worker deserves his keep. Whatever town or village you enter, look for some worthy person in it, and stay with him until you leave. And when you go into a house, salute it by saying: Peace on this house.

Francis cried, 'That is what I want, what I am looking for, what I desire to do from the bottom of my heart.' Brimming over with joy, he removed his shoes, threw away his staff and kept only a single tunic which he tied with a rope instead of a belt. He decorated this garment with an image of the Cross and made it so rough that it mortified his flesh, flesh of vice and sin, made it so poor and ugly that no one in the world would envy it.

It was the 'third year of the conversion' of Francis, on 12 October 1208 or 24 February 1209. Francis was 26 or 27 years old. From a convert he became a missionary. Saint Francis had been born; the Franciscans were yet to be born.

From the first to the second Rule

Thus, Francis began to preach 'with his voice that was like a burning fire'. He preached in Assisi, in or near the church where he had received his religious education as a small child and where he would first be buried – San Giorgio, today incorporated into Santa Chiara. His first convert in that year of 1209 was a simple and pious man about whom we know nothing. Then a rich man came, Bernard of Quintavalle, who sold all his goods and gave the money to the poor and joined Francis. The third was another man from Assisi, a lawyer and canon, who had studied in Bologna, Peter Catani, who would be Francis's successor as head of the Order in 1220. The fourth was Brother Giles.

From that period began the itinerant preaching. From time to time, we will note a particular stage marked by a well-known or significant episode, and we will dwell upon the furthest points of his journey –

towards Rome or outside Italy. But, except for brief retreats, Francis and his companions were now always on the road, preaching in the cities and the villages. His prime domain was Italy, from Rome to Verona, but mainly Umbria and the Marches. He accomplished his first mission, according to *The Legend of the Three Companions*, in the march of Ancona, which was to be a heartland of Franciscanism, the cradle of the *Fioretti*. Later, when there were eight brothers, Francis, who always sent them out in twos, as Christ did with the apostles (Mark 6:7; Luke 1:1), and who himself always travelled with a brother, sent Brother Bernard and Brother Giles to Santiago di Compostella. He and his companion went into the Rieti valley, whence they returned with new recruits, among them Brother Angelo who, with Brother Leo and Brother Ruffino, made up the team of the 'three companions'. Thus, like the Apostles, there were twelve of them, who met again at the Portiuncula in the winter of 1209–10.

Successes counterbalanced failures in these early days, some of the former sufficiently encouraging to confirm Francis in his mission, some of the latter so clear-cut as to worry him. During the first campaign in the Marches, people took him and his companions for maniacs. On the way to Compostella, Bernard and Giles were very badly received in Florence. If Thomas of Celano remains silent on these difficulties and emphasises certain successes, the 'three companions', no doubt exaggerating in the opposite sense, speak of total failure. There was another cause for concern: Guy, the bishop of Assisi who had protected Francis at the time of his conversion, became, if not hostile, at least wary. Francis must have had recourse to all his powers of persuasion to convince him of the legitimacy of his activities and way of life. To curtail these threats, Francis decided to go to Rome with the eleven brothers and ask the Pope to approve his conduct and that of his brothers.

Francis and Innocent III

This trip to Rome poses difficult problems for historians. First, was the approval that Francis wanted from the Pope for a 'Rule' and thus for the foundation of a new 'Order'? The text submitted to Innocent III has been lost, and what Thomas of Celano says is very vague: 'Francis wrote for himself and his brothers, present and future, simply and succinctly, a guide for living and a rule that was essentially composed of quotes from the Holy Gospels whose perfection he desired only ardently to realise.' 'Vitae formam et regulam': it does seem that the biographer of 1228 added the word *regula* on his own initiative and that the truth lies in the words *formula vitae* – a simple formulary composed of a few sentences from the Gospels guiding the life and apostolate of the brothers.

Second, what was the attitude of Innocent III? Three interviews seem to have taken place between Francis and the Pope, and apparently it was difficult for the Poverello to extract approval from the pontiff.

What sort of men were these two? They were both pastors, whose personality, function and experience were the opposite in almost every way. Innocent III was imbued with the pessimistic spirituality of the monastic tradition; the work he wrote, *De contemptu mundi* (*On the Misery of the Human Condition*) is the exact opposite of Francis's declaration of love for all creatures. Although Francis aspired only to heaven, he aspired to it through them. Even if Innocent III was not the 'political' pope that many historians see in him, he was convinced of the primacy of spiritual power over temporal power; better yet, he was convinced that the vicar of Christ possesses the two swords, the two powers. Francis said,

> May all the brothers beware not to show any attitude of power or superiority, especially among themselves. The Lord says in the Gospel, '*The princes of nations dominate them and the great exercise their power over them.*' It will not be so among the brothers, but *anyone who would want to be superior among them, let him be their servant and their slave, and he who would be superior, let him be minor.*[9]

For Francis, enemies do not exist outside ourselves; they are our vices and our sins and, in any case, one must not judge others. Innocent III saw the Church assailed by troops of enemies, the princes who called themselves Christians and on whom in turn (on the Emperor, the King of France, and the King of England) he declared excommunication and anathema, these heretics who were swarming – the Poor Men of Lyon, who became Waldensians, and those Humiliates, who were only partly obedient, those Cathars and Albigensians, against whom he called for a crusade and prepared the Inquisition. Now – this layman in rags who came before the fat, luxurious and arrogant curia, to preach this scandal, the integral implementation of the

Gospel, the realisation of the Gospel in its entirety – was he not, in the eyes of the Pope, on the road to heresy, if not already a heretic? There would thus have been an initial stormy interview. This man with 'his miserable tunic, his unkempt hair and his enormous black eyebrows', Innocent III took him or pretended to take him for a swineherd: 'Don't bother me with your Rule. Go back to your pigs and preach all the sermons you want to them.' Francis ran to a pigsty, covered himself with dung and returned before the Pope. 'Lord, now that I have done what you commanded, have the goodness in your turn to grant me what I request.' The Pope, concluded the English chronicler Matthew Paris, 'reflected, and then regretted that he had received him so badly, and having sent him off to wash, promised him another audience.'

What seems certain is that, after a first hostile reception, either from the Pope himself or from the curia, Francis prepared for the new meeting with Innocent. He found people to introduce him, support and protect him. The mediator was Bishop Guy of Assisi and, through his intervention, Cardinal John of Saint Paul, a member of the Colonna family, finally agreed to pave the way for Francis to meet the Pope. However, when Francis was able to submit the text of his 'Rule' to Innocent III, the Pope was alarmed by its severity. The Gospel in its entirety – what madness! But Cardinal John of Saint Paul found the right argument to sway the pontiff, an argument both religious and political. 'If we reject this poor man's request on such a pretext, would we not be saying that the Gospel is impracticable and so blaspheming Christ its author?' Innocent III, moved but not convinced, merely said to Francis, 'My son, go and pray to God to show us His will; once we shall know it, we will be able to reply to you in all security.'

Francis and his allies took advantage of this new delay, and God manifested his will. Innocent III had a dream: he saw the Lateran basilica leaning as though ready to crumble. A 'small and ugly' religious was supporting it on his back and preventing it from crashing down. The man in his dream could only be Francis. He would save the Church.

And so Innocent III approved the text that Francis submitted to him, but in such a way as to hedge himself with many safeguards. He gave only verbal approval, not written. He demanded that the brothers obey Francis and that Francis promise obedience to the popes. Without conferring major Orders on them, he had all those who were lay tonsured and probably made Francis a deacon. Finally, he only gave them permission to preach, that is, to give people moral exhortations.

Francis was not asking for more. 'Go, my brothers,' Innocent III said, according to Thomas of Celano, as he blessed them,

> go with the Lord and may the Lord inspire you, preach penance to all. When the almighty Lord will have made you increase in numbers and in grace, come back joyfully to me and I will grant you more favours and I will entrust you more confidently with greater missions.

Reading between the lines of this optimistic account, it appears that while Francis had managed to obtain the essentials, he had not dissipated the Pope's distrust. And then Francis's companions, who had hastened to leave Rome, stopped in a remote spot in the Spoleto valley and questioned their own vocations: 'Rather than go and preach to people, wouldn't it be better to become hermits?' Francis once again needed all the resources of his impassioned discourse to persuade them not to shrink from their mission.

Sources other than Thomas of Celano cast greater doubt on whether Saint Francis was satisfied with his trip to Rome. Matthew Paris, following the Benedictine Roger of Wendover, dates a famous episode in Francis's life to his return from Rome, in the valley of Spoleto: the sermon to the birds. But he gives a rather different interpretation of it from the elegiac sense in which it is presented – at a later date – by the official biographers of Francis. He says that the saint, wounded by his reception by the Romans, by their vices and vileness, called the birds from the sky, even the most aggressive, those with dangerous beaks, birds of prey and crows, to teach *them* the good news, not the miserable Romans. It is easy to see that this anecdote comes from Revelation 19: 17–18:

> Then I saw an angel standing in the sun, and with a loud voice he called to all the birds that fly in midheaven, 'Come, gather for the great supper of God, to eat the flesh of kings, the flesh of captains, the flesh of the mighty, the flesh of horses and their riders – flesh of all, both free and slave, both small and great.'

This invective sounds quite unlike the gentle Francis, and it shows that the extremist Franciscan party may have wanted to have the Order's founder assimilate Rome and the Church with accursed Babylon. The iconography of the thirteenth century preserved this memory: the images representing Francis preaching to the birds more or less copied other contemporary images showing the angel of the Apocalypse calling birds to the spoils – until Giotto definitively imposed the idyllic interpretation of the scene (see Plates 13–16). In any case, behind this tendentious and forced interpretation, it would seem that Francis could not have kept a happy memory of his relations with Rome and Innocent III. This could be an argument against the unproved allegation that he attended the Fourth Lateran Council of 1215.

Back in Assisi, Francis and his companions went to settle on a plain at a bend in a meandering stream, the Rivo Torto. There they occupied an abandoned cabin, Francis reminding his brothers that 'one gets to heaven more quickly from a hut than from a palace'. They divided their time between caring for lepers, manual labour, begging and preaching, notably in Assisi. After a few months they had to leave their cabin because, according to Thomas of Celano, a peasant invited his donkey to enter the hovel to chase away its denizens, but more probably because the arrival of new brothers had made the tiny lodging uninhabitable. The bishop and canons declined to take responsibility, but the abbot of the Benedictine monastery of Monte Subasio conceded to Francis the chapel of the Portiuncula and a patch of adjoining land. The same life continued in the small community, which grew little by little. Among the new brothers in the year 1210–11 were Brother Ruffino, 'who prayed even in his sleep', Brother Juniper, 'the perfect imitator of the crucified Jesus', the paradigmatic 'jongleur of God' who has been called the 'typical Franciscan', Brother Masseo with his sturdy common sense, Brother Lucido, 'who never stayed more than a month in the same place, because we have no permanent dwelling here below', and finally, the pure and ingenuous Brother Leo, the most stubbornly loyal to Saint Francis, who made him his confessor because he was a priest, and who called him 'brother little lamb of God'.

Saint Clare

If the Portiuncula became Francis's favourite residence from the end of 1210, nevertheless he did often leave it, either to go and preach in Assisi, Umbria, central and northern Italy, and the land of the Infidels, or else to take solitary retreats in hermitages – the Carceri on the slopes of Subasio, on an island on Lake Trasimene, at Monte Casale, near

Borgo San Sepulcro, at Fonte Colombo near Rieti, in a place near Orte, at Poggio Bustone, in an oratory near Siena, at Celle near Cortona, at Sant' Urbano near Narni, at Sarteano near Chiusi, and finally at La Verna. He and his brothers were not always well received. In 1211 the Bolognese greeted Brother Bernard of Quintavalle with volleys of stones and heaped sarcasm on him in the great square of the city. But in 1212 Francis made a choice recruit. A noble young lady of Assisi, inspired by the sermons of the saint, escaped from her family home with a friend on the night of Palm Sunday and took refuge in the Portiuncula where Francis cut their hair and dressed them in homespun robes like his, and then led them to the Benedictine monastery of San Paolo de Bastia, a few kilometres away, in the marshes of Insula Romana. After a few days, they went to a safer place, the monastery of Sant' Angelo, where other Benedictines were living on Monte Subasio above Carceri. Chiara and Pacifica were joined there by Chiara's younger sister, Agnese, whose hair Francis also cut. Some time afterwards, Bishop Guido gave the chapel of San Damiano to Chiara and the 'Poor Ladies', who would later be called the Poor Clares, as the Franciscans would be named the 'Friars Minor'. Thus, in the tradition of monasticism with parallel branches for men and women, inaugurated by Saint Benedict and Saint Scholastica, Francis and Clare always followed a common path until death. 'Since you have become the daughters and servants of the heavenly Father and the spouses of the Holy Spirit in choosing to live according to the perfection of the Holy Gospels, I promise to watch over you always, as I do over my own brothers', wrote Francis to the Poor Ladies. He kept his word and was always obeyed and cherished by them as he was by his brothers.

Miracles and peregrinations

The year 1212 was one of effervescence and hope for Christianity. The Christian kings of the Iberian Peninsula united their forces against the Moslems and, on 14 July 1212, defeated the Infidels in the most brilliant victory of the Reconquista at Las Navas de Tolosa. From June to September, waves of young people from France and Germany who wanted to go to the Holy Land arrived in northern Italy. This was the misnamed 'Children's Crusade', which ran into a thousand material and moral problems, including the hostility of the majority of the church hierarchy. It disbanded sadly. Like its members, Francis and one of his brothers embarked on a ship leaving for Syria. But the ship was blown by unfavourable winds onto the Dalmatian coast, whence Francis and his companion returned to Ancona with great difficulty. Penniless, they secretly climbed on board a boat where the crew, on discovering them, threatened to make trouble for them. They escaped this fate only because the saint calmed a storm and also increased his meagre provisions enough to feed all the sailors, who were faced with starvation because of a long period without wind.

The journey, however, had merely been postponed. Two years later, in 1214, he set off once again to preach to the Saracens, this time for Morocco, where he thought he would find an audience with the Sultan, who must have been shattered by his defeat at Las Navas. But Francis fell ill in Spain and had to return to Italy. He would succeed – partially – in his enterprise only in 1219, in Egypt.

However, the companions of Saint Francis were ever more numerous, and their reputation was spreading. Among the newcomers were Giovanni Parenti in Florence and Brother Elias in Cortona, both future ministers general. An increasing number of miracles were attributed to Francis. At Ascoli, he healed the sick and converted thirty people at once, both clergy and laity; at Arezzo, the reins of a bridle that he had held in his hands healed a woman dying in labour; at Città della Pieve, one of his followers healed the sick by touching them with a rope that Francis had used as a belt; at Toscanella, he healed a lame man, and at Narni a paralytic; he exorcised the possessed at San Gemini, between Todi and Terni, and at Città di Castello. Near Bevagna he is believed to have preached to the birds, and at Gubbio, according to the *Fioretti*, to have influenced 'Brother Wolf' to stop being vicious. The man who had been jeered now inspired not just curiosity but reverence and enthusiasm wherever he went. When his arrival was announced in a town or village, all the people ran up to him with cries of 'Here is the saint!' ('Ecco il santo!') Bells were rung, people went before him waving branches and singing, he was given bread to bless, and bits of his tunic were cut off. In 1213, he preached at a festival in a castle of Montefeltro. The minstrel of God blended his voice with those of the profane troubadours. A member of the audience, Count Orlando de Chiusi in Casentino, was moved, and he made Francis a gift of the Mount La Verna so that he could establish a hermitage there for himself and his companions.

The Fourth Lateran Council

In 1215, the Church experienced a great event: Pope Innocent III called a council in Saint John Lateran, the fourth to be held in that church. The council decided on a new crusade and established the foundations of a church reform. This timid *aggiornamento* tended generally to coincide with Saint Francis's wishes, and the Pope chose as the emblem of the reform the sign of the tau, which marked the foreheads of the righteous and which was dear to Francis (he signed his letters with it and painted it on the walls of the hermitages). For these reasons there has been some interest in defining the exact connections between the council and Saint Francis. It has been claimed that he was present and met Saint Dominic there. Nothing proves this. But Innocent III, Francis and Dominic, in a different spirit and in different styles, sought to bring solutions to the same problem: to open new paths to salvation for humanity in a changing world. On the basis of this common objective, the conclusion was later drawn that actual meetings took place, whose purpose was to paper over the divergences separating the Roman curia from the two saints or, if not them, at least their spiritual heirs. That the council contained a threat for Francis, Dominic and their companions is obvious. Canon 13 strictly forbade the founding of new Orders, and Canon 10 provided for bishops to be assisted by auxiliaries 'not only to preach, but to hear confessions, distribute penances and for everything else related to the salvation of souls'. This role for auxiliaries, who were closely subordinated to the hierarchy, obviously ran counter to the intentions of Dominic and Francis. They attempted to avert the threat in different ways. By adopting the Rule of Saint Augustine for his Preachers, who were organised in a confraternity of regular canons, in 1216 Dominic succeeded in founding his Order under the fiction of simply continuing an existing tradition. Francis proceeded more discreetly. He was anxious not to turn his companions into a true Order, so as to retain greater flexibility for them, and he felt that by having the laity and clergy coexist, he could more easily build a bridge between the Church and the laity. No doubt, he was using Innocent III's verbal approval as grounds for considering that his brothers had already been recognised and were not affected by the council's decisions.

However, to consolidate their position with the faithful and the hierarchy, it has been alleged that in 1216 he requested and obtained from the new Pope Honorius III the indulgence of the Portiuncula, that is, a plenary indulgence for anyone who visited the sanctuary on the anniversary of its dedication, 2 August – an inordinate privilege that put the oratory of Francis on the same plane as Rome, the Holy Land and Santiago de Compostella. Whether this happed is very dubious, because no reliable document provides confirmation of the existence of this indulgence before 1277, and its legend must have sprung from the crowds of pilgrims who were attracted to the place from very early on.

In any case, Francis gave his companions some degree of organisation, rendered necessary by their growing numbers and expanded activities. It is very difficult to give specific details on the periodical meetings of the first companions of Saint Francis, to whom the name 'chapter' has been given (with some exaggeration). It seems that as long as there were only a few brothers, Francis asked them to return twice a year to the Portiuncula, at Pentecost and Michaelmas. But when their numbers increased and their range of activity expanded, it became impossible for Francis to convene them more than once a year. This was probably already the case as early as 1216. The meeting of 1217 took on special importance as it was there that Francis decided that the brothers should preach outside Italy. Was it this meeting that is described in the *Fioretti* in the highly improbable chapter about rush mats, where the assembly of the brothers (who had built huts of willow-trellis for the occasion) is portrayed as a joyful and simple village fair. Francis then himself decided to leave for France with Brother Masseo. On his way through Florence, he went to greet Cardinal Ugolino, who was there preaching for the crusade. Was it then – or earlier – that the Cardinal was convinced by Francis? From that time on Ugolino lavished both practical advice and counsels of prudence on Francis and his companions. And, to begin with, he persuaded Francis to abandon the trip to France. Did this well-informed prelate fear the spread of enthusiasm for Franciscanism in France or did he understand that Francis would be risking a great deal by leaving his bases without consolidating them? The missionaries who had left Italy had in fact achieved nothing and were particularly badly received in Germany.

In 1219, however, Francis took up his old plan: to go to the Infidels, convert them or be martyred. Having sailed from Ancona on 24 June, he was present at the taking of Damietta by the crusaders on 5 November, and was disgusted by their greedy and bloodthirsty behaviour. He obtained a fruitless interview with Sultan Malik al-Kamil, and went to Palestine where he may have visited the Holy Places. In Palestine, he learned that five of the brothers who had left for Morocco had suffered martyrdom there. Already distressed by this news, he then received an emissary demanding his return to Italy, where the brothers, in his absence, were going through a serious crisis. In the summer of 1220, he set sail again and, in the autumn, arrived in Venice. It seems that he travelled directly to Rome. In any case, he realised that he could not take the situation back in hand without obtaining the support of the papal curia and without, consequently, making them some concessions. In the decisions taken from 1221 to 1223 on the reorganisation of his movement, it is sometimes difficult to distinguish between what Saint Francis wanted and what was imposed on him.

What had happened? On the one hand, the extremists had given free rein to extravagant tendencies: becoming pure vagabonds, associating with women to the point of 'eating with them, from the same bowl', and forming communities of lepers of both genders. On the other hand, the latitudinarians wanted, on the contrary, to distance themselves from rigorism and build beautiful stone churches, pursue and encourage studies, and ask for favours from the Roman curia. In one case, at least, Francis reacted ruthlessly and quickly. Going from Venice to Rome, he passed through Bologna, where Brother John of Staccia had established a house of study. He chased everyone away, even the sick, and cursed John of Staccia. A series of measures was taken, more or less in agreement with his wishes. One year of noviciate was required of anyone who wanted to enter the community from then on. A representative of the Holy See became the 'protector, governor and corrector of the fraternity'. This was Cardinal Ugolino. Francis ceded the administrative leadership of the community to Peter Catani, who died soon after on 10 March 1221, and was replaced by Brother Elias. Finally, Francis, who had remained the spiritual head of the community, had to transform it into a genuine Order and give it a firm Rule to replace the 'formula' of 1210.

Francis presented his Rule to the 'chapter' of 1221. It met with so many reservations, as much from some of the brothers as from the representative of the Roman curia, that the decision was taken to submit it to the cardinal protector. In the meanwhile, to accommodate the crowds of lay people who wanted to join the Order and probably at the suggestion of Ugolino, drawing inspiration from what had been instituted among the Humiliates, a 'third order' was created. This Third Order certainly corresponded to Francis's desire to keep his fraternity as a small community of the pure. According to Thomas of Celano, he sighed, 'There are too many Minors! Ah! Let the time come when people, instead of meeting Minors by the side of every field, complain of seeing too few.' The *Fioretti* has him say 'Don't be in such a hurry' to the people of Cannara who wanted to leave everything and follow him. But the Third Order, in the form that it was given, corresponded chiefly to the desires of the Holy See to contain the Franciscan tide and to take advantage of it by diverting it into a combined secular and religious militia at the service of its spiritual and temporal interests. As early as December 1221, Pope Honorius III used the many Franciscan tertiaries of Faenza against the imperial party. The Third Order became an instrument of Guelphic politics. It may not be a coincidence that the first community of the Franciscan Third Order was probably founded in March 1221, in Florence (the chief Guelphic city), while Francis and Cardinal Ugolino were staying there. In any case, the Rule for the Third Order, dry and legalistic, composed in 1221 and approved by the Pope, bears little of Francis's personal stamp. It was perhaps also at that time that Francis approved the teaching inaugurated by a Portuguese brother known as Anthony of Padua in the same convent in Bologna from which he had just chased John of Staccia and his companions, mainly because they had engaged in study. But the letter from Francis to Anthony that supports this assumption is not necessarily authentic.

The *Regula bullata*

Nevertheless, the Pope and Cardinal Ugolino had asked Saint Francis to revise the drafted Rule of 1221. Saint Francis retired to the hermitage of Fonte Colombo near Rieti, in the company of Brother Leo and a brother who had some background in law, Brother Bonizzo. The revisions must have seemed insufficient to Elias as he lost the text entrusted to him by Francis, who then started the work again with Brother Leo. It was a difficult task: Francis was discouraged and sometimes even bitter. The saint curtly dismissed any brothers who came to bother him by asking him to introduce into the text tendencies contrary to his intentions. Finally, the new Rule was ready in the spring or summer of 1223. It was sent to Rome, where Cardinal Ugolino revised it again, and it was approved by Pope Honorius III in the bull of 29 November

1223, *Solet annuere*, whence its name *Regula bullata*. Most of the quotations from the Gospel in the Rule of 1221 were omitted from the new text, and the lyrical passages were removed and replaced with legalistic formulas. An article that authorised the brothers to disobey unworthy superiors was deleted. Also removed was everything about the care to be given to lepers and all the prescriptions meant to make the brothers practise strict poverty. The Rule no longer insisted on the necessity of manual labour and no longer prohibited the brothers from having books.

Francis, with death in his soul, accepted this deformed Rule. The biographers call this period of his life, at the end of 1223, the time of the 'great temptation' – temptation to completely abandon the new Order, if not orthodoxy. Obedience – the obedience to the Church that he had made a strict precept – suddenly seemed laughable to him. 'The obedient man', he said, according to Saint Bonaventure (taking up a tendentious passage of Thomas of Celano),

> must be like a corpse that can be placed anywhere, without protesting. If he is dressed in purple, he only seems more livid. If he is seated at a desk like a doctor, he certainly does not raise his head, but lets it fall down on his chest.

Then he resigned himself and became peaceful: 'Poor little man, the Lord said to him, why be so sad? Is your Order not mine? Is it not I who am its supreme pastor? So stop your grieving and instead take care of your own salvation.'

Thus Francis came to consider his own salvation as independent of the Order sprung from him, indeed, despite him. He serenely followed his path towards death.

Towards death

Thomas of Celano divided his *Vita prima* of Saint Francis into two very chronologically disproportionate parts. In fact, the second part covers only the last two years of Francis's life, from 1224 to 1226. At this point Francis retired from the world until his final illness made him return to it. He had, according to his biographer's words, 'left the secular crowds who every day hastened full of devotion to hear and see him'. Thomas of Celano thus ended his first part on a long note of gentleness and sweetness, portraying Francis's love as overflowing: his love for the poor, whose bundles of firewood and burdens he bore on his shoulders, for animals, even snakes, and especially for sheep and lambs that he prevented from being sold and killed by buying them back with the gift of his coat, for all creation – from worms and bees to harvests, vineyards, flowers, forests, stones and the four elements. And the famous crib scene of Greccio was the crowning moment of this lyrical finale.

At the end of Francis's life, we can find other movements and another orchestration. After the 'great temptation' came a long period of peace in which episodes of overflowing tenderness and sublimated suffering alternated and mingled, leading Francis, through a slow and protracted death agony, to his last breath.

The first episode was Christmas 1223. Francis replied to the invitation from one of the nobles who had been influenced by him, Giovanni Velita, the lord of Greccio, who intended to celebrate the Nativity among the caves and hermitages of a steep mountain and asked his friend to reconstruct the crib of Bethlehem, as his poetic imagination inspired him.

> I wish to remember the child who was born in Bethlehem and to see with my own eyes the hardships of his needy childhood, how he rested in the crib, and how, between a cow and a donkey, he was laid in the hay.

On Christmas Eve, men and women from all around climbed the mountain with so many candles and torches that the night was completely lit up by it. They sang; the forest carried their voices; the rocks reverberated with them. Mass was celebrated. The saint of God was near the crib; he was singing the Gospel; he was preaching 'with his fiery voice, with his gentle voice, with his clear voice, with his ringing voice'. He proclaimed the eternal rewards. A man in the audience had a vision: he suddenly saw the child lying in the crib and Francis bending over him to wake him up. Greccio was a new Bethlehem.

After spending the winter and the spring of 1224 at Greccio, Francis went to the Portiuncula for the general chapter of June, the last for which he was present, and then travelled to another hermitage, that of La Verna. He took with him only a few brothers, those dearest to his heart, 'the three companions' Leo, Angelo and Ruffino, along with Sylvester, Illuminato, Masseo and, perhaps, Bonizzo. Having arrived with them in the wilderness, he often left them for solitary retreats. He gave himself up to contemplation. One day, he opened the only book that he used to read, the only book he had brought with him, the Gospels, and he fell upon the story of Christ's passion. And on another day, perhaps 14 September, his last vision appeared above him: a man with six wings like a seraph, with open arms and joined feet, fixed to a cross. And as he meditated on this vision, full of both joy and sadness, bleeding holes opened on his hands and feet, and a wound appeared on his side. Francis had completed his path towards the imitation of Christ. He was the first Christian to bear the stigmata, 'the crucified servant of the crucified Lord'. The event made him as embarrassed as it made him joyful. He tried to hide his stigmata, wrapping his feet and hands with bandages. During his lifetime, according to Thomas of Celano, only Brother Elias saw them and Brother Ruffino touched them. On his death, those surrounding him rushed to his body and the number of people claiming to have seen Francis's stigmata grew steadily throughout the thirteenth century.

In the autumn of 1224, feeling confirmed in his mission by the stigmata, Francis recommenced his rounds, travelling by donkey. But his infirmities increased. He nearly went blind and he suffered from terrible headaches. Saint Clare, to whom he paid a visit in San Damiano, kept him with her for a few weeks to care for him. He built himself a willow hut in the garden and experienced one of his last periods of earthly peacefulness there. People like to think that he composed the 'Canticle of the Creatures' there, the song of all created beings. Brother Elias managed to persuade him to consult the doctors of the Pope, whose court then resided at Rieti. He accompanied him like a mother, according to Thomas of Celano, and like a supervisor, according to many historians. In Rieti, Francis lodged either in the bishop's palace or, as reported in the *Legenda antiqua*, in the house of 'Tabald the Saracen', probably a Moslem doctor of the Pope. The doctors' knowledge was in vain: Francis's condition deteriorated. The brothers of Siena invited him to stay with them, saying that they could take care of him and perhaps heal him. But, on the contrary, his illness worsened to such a degree that he dictated his will to them (of this Thomas de Celano breathes not a word) and Brother Elias hastened to his bedside. Francis improved. He then left Siena with Brother Elias for the hermitage of Celle, near Cortona. But there, illness seized him with such violence that Francis asked to be taken back to Assisi, in fact to the Portiuncula.

But if it was Brother Elias's wish that Francis should die in Assisi, the cradle of Franciscanism, there was great danger in his staying at the Portiuncula. Indeed, in the early thirteenth century, the mentality and behaviour of the masses and of individuals towards characters reputed to be saintly had not changed since the end of the fourth century, when the people of Tours stole the body of Saint Martin from the people of Poitiers. At the end of the tenth century, the Catalans thought of killing off the sick Saint Romuald so as to keep his relics. Around the dying Francis, covetousness lay in wait for the holy corpse. The great fear of the people of Assisi was of their traditional enemies, the people of Perugia. Now, the Portiuncula, in the plains, was at the mercy of a raid by the Perugians. The dying man was therefore transported inside the ramparts, into the episcopal palace, where Francis would be safe both from the Perugians and from any religious mavericks. Francis felt less at ease than ever in the palaces of the Church. He finally succeeded in having himself moved to the Portiuncula. He was watched over by the brothers and guarded by relays of armed men of Assisi. Francis had reached the last stages of the Imitation of Christ, and had already received the ultimate seal, the stigmata. On 2 October, he proceeded to the last supper. He blessed and broke the bread and distributed it to his brothers. The next day, 3 October 1226, he asked for 'The Canticle of the Creatures' to be sung to him, for the Passion from the Gospel according to St John to be read, and for a hair shirt covered with ashes to be placed on the floor. At that moment, one of the brothers who were present suddenly saw his soul, like a star, rise straight for heaven. He was 45 or 46 years old.

Everything happened very quickly afterwards. There was a stampede on the body, to see the stigmata and to touch the holy relic. The funeral, on 4 October, was simple, with a stop at San Damiano, where Saint Clare covered the body of her celestial friend with tears and kisses, and a temporary burial at San Giorgio. Then, on 17 July 1228, less than two years after Francis's death, canonisation was pronounced by the papacy, which, although not in the habit of hurrying, did make haste to curtail the controversies surrounding this saint who was still troublesome. By this time Cardinal Ugolino had become Pope Gregory IX, and the tribute he paid to his protégé contained a mixture of veneration and political scheming. Then, on 25 May 1230, there was the insult of the inhumation in the crypt of the ostentatious basilica that Brother Elias had had built in violation of Francis's ethos. The final betrayal would be the horrible basilica of Santa Maria degli Angeli with which, after 1569, post-Tridentine Catholicism would crown and smother the humble and authentic Portiuncula.

The works and the legacy

Saint Francis did not write much. Even if we possessed the first Rule and the lost letters and poems, all these riches would occupy one slender volume. The edition published by the Franciscans of Quaracchi is divided into three parts: (1) *The Admonitions* and the Rules; (2) the letters; and (3) the prayers. On the pretext of publishing only the works in Latin, the Quaracchi fathers mutilated the written work of Saint Francis by excising a vital masterpiece, 'The Canticle of the Creatures', written in Italian. Thus, it is advisable to improve and complete the presentation as Vittorio Facchinetti and Giacomo Cambell have done in Italian (I *Legislazione serafica*; II *La direttive del Padre*; III *La corrispondenza di un santo*; IV *Inni e preghiere*, 'Il cantico di frate Sole' included) and, in French, Alexandre Masseron (I *Le législateur*; II *Le messager*; III *L'ami*; IV *Le Saint en prière*; V *Le Poète*).

But underneath the variety of their outer forms, all these short works are only contributions to a single legacy: the spiritual training of his brothers and, beyond that, the communication of a message to humanity. Francis was not a writer – he was a missionary completing, with a few writings, a message whose essence he had expressed through the spoken word and through example.

Between the Rule of 1221, which was not approved, and the Rule still in use today by the Minors, which was confirmed in 1223 by papal bull, there are differences, whose main points we have summarised and which include the effects of condensing into twelve rather dry articles a text of twenty-three articles that are rich in evangelical quotations and effusions.

The exordium confirms the requirement for the Minors to respect the three rules of obedience, poverty and chastity. The goal that is assigned to them in the first Rule is to 'follow the teachings and the example of Our Lord Jesus Christ' and, more abstractly in the second, 'to observe the Holy Gospel of Our Lord Jesus Christ'. The ministers general of the Order would obey the Pope; the brothers would obey the ministers general.

Then follow the conditions of entry into the Order – a novitiate lasting for one year, the giving of all personal possessions to the poor – and a description of the clothing: one habit with a hood, one habit without a hood, one belt, one pair of breeches, and all made of coarse fabric. The second Rule adds shoes to this, if necessary.

The *opus Dei* is brief. For the clergy there is the divine office and the breviary, for the laity twenty-four *Pater* at matins, five at lauds, seven for prime, tierce, sext and nones, twelve at vespers and seven for compline, and the prayer for the dead. The prohibition against possessing any books other than the breviary and the psalter – and only for those who could read – disappears from the second Rule. Of the two fasts imposed by the first Rule, from All Souls' Day to Christmas, and from Epiphany to Easter, the second, in the second Rule, was reduced to Lent, the fast from Epiphany to Lent becoming optional. Fasting on Fridays was added to this. But all food taboos were prohibited.

The relationships between the ministers and the other brothers were both more succinct and more strict in the second Rule. The brothers' duty to disobey any ministers ordering something contrary to the Rule or to conscience, 'for there is no disobedience where there is crime or sin' ('Quia illa obedientia non est, in qua delictum vel peccatum committitur'), disappeared, in the same way as the prohibition of calling anyone *priore*, as everyone was supposed to be called *frati minore*. The ministers were to order the brothers to do only that which is contrary neither to the good of their soul nor to the Rule, but the brothers were committed to complete obedience to them. The duty for all, ministers and brothers, to wash one another's feet also vanished.

The absolute prohibition against receiving money was maintained, but without the litany of details and curses of the first text and with the addition of the possibility for the ministers and custodians to receive, through the intermediary of 'amici spirituali', enough to take care of the sick and to dress the brothers 'according to the regions, the weather and cold climates' ('secondo i luoghi, i tempi ed i paesi freddi').

The regulations concerning work were equally weakened. This was no longer required of everyone, but only permitted to brothers 'to whom the Lord has conceded the grace to work' ('cui il Signore ha concesso la grazia del lavoro'). Begging was exalted to the skies: it was the sublime peak of this very high poverty that has made you, my very dear brothers, the heirs and kings of the kingdom of heaven.

(la vetta sublime de quell'altissima povertà, che ha fatto voi, fratelli miei carissimi, eredi e re del regno dei cieli.)

But it was taken out of the context that, in the first Rule, gave all its meaning to the practice. This context was twofold: social and apostolic. On the one hand, begging placed the brothers physically among the poor:

They must be happy to be among people of low condition and of no account, among the poor and the weak, the sick, the lepers and the street beggars.

(E debbono essere felici quando si trovano tra gente dappoco e tenuta in nessun conto, tra i poveri e i deboli, gli infermi, i lebbrosi e i mendicanti della via.)

This whole procession of the involuntary poor that gave meaning to voluntary poverty disappeared from the second text. Similarly, the christological and apostolic reference that said of Jesus, 'and he was poor and a pilgrim and lived off alms himself and with him the Holy Virgin and his disciples' ('e fu povero e pellegrino e visse di elemosine lui stesso e con lui la beata virgine ed i suoi discepoli') gave way to a vague allusion to Christ's poverty: 'the Lord for love for us made himself poor in this world' ('il Signore per amor nostro si fece egli stesso povero in questo mondo'). Of all the details concerning poverty while travelling ('When the brothers go travelling in the world, they may bring nothing for the journey, no purse, no bag, no money, no stick' ('Quando i frati vanno per il mondo, non portino nulla per il viaggio, nè borsa, nè bisaccia, nè pane, nè denaro, nè bastone'), there remained only the prohibition against horse riding, except in cases of illness or dire necessity.

The conditions for electing the minister general, reserved for the provincial ministers and the custodians, and the convocation of the general chapter at Pentecost, normally every three years, were specified; however, the electors could depose a general minister who seemed unsuited to fulfilling his office and serving the common good of the brothers.

Preaching, ordered to all the brothers in the first Rule, was strictly regulated in the second. It could take place only in dioceses where the bishops authorised it. It had to be subordinated to an examination and to a licence granted by the general minister. Preaching was limited to being brief and discussing moral and instructive subjects only – not theology, dogma or any subjects connected with church jurisdiction,

> for the use and the education of the people, addressing them on the vices and the virtues, on punishment and glory, in short sermons.
>
> (per utilità e edificazione del popolo, parlando loro dei vizi e delle virtù, della pena e della gloria, con brevita di sermone.)

The detailed and severe condemnations concerning contacts with women and fornication were replaced by a brief article mainly forbidding the brothers to enter, without special permission, the monasteries of cloistered nuns.

The long article on missionary work – highly recommended among the Saracens and other infidels – was reduced to four lines, advising the ministers to grant this permission only with great prudence; and the second Rule ends by mentioning that a cardinal had been given to the Order by the Pope 'as the governor, protector and corrector of this fraternity' ('come governatore, protettore e correttore di questa fraternità'). In the last line, however, Saint Francis was able to quote 'the Holy Gospel of Our Lord Jesus Christ' ('Il santo Vangelo del Signor Nostro Gesù Cristo').

To these two essential texts must be added the *Admonitions*, *Della religiosa abitazione nell'eremo* ('A Rule for Hermitages'), the *Testament* and the 'Short Testament'.

The twenty-eight *Admonitions* are very simple little spiritual texts summarising the teachings on the practice of the religious life that Francis gave orally to his brothers and that had not found a place in the Rule, being more recommendations than compulsory prescriptions. This is a short treatise on good and bad religious – or, as it has been called, 'Saint Francis's sermon on the mount'.

The text on the life of the brothers in the hermitages also completes the Rule, which remains almost silent on these retreats into solitude that corresponded to a hermit tradition valued and practised by Francis and most of his companions. It mainly decides on the relationship between active life and contemplative life during the course of these retreats. In groups of three or four, the brothers should divide themselves between two 'mothers' leading the active life of Martha, and one or two 'children' leading the contemplative life of Mary Magdalene.

The *Testament*, probably written in Siena during the winter of 1225–26, is an essential text. Francis wanted to make it a complement to the Rule, with the same status as the law of the Order, something that Pope Gregory IX was quick to annul as early as 1230 in the bull *Quo elongati*. Francis seems to have sought to reintroduce into it a certain number of the principles or prescriptions that had been removed or weakened in the Rule of 1223. It has been said – as though Francis had guessed that his intentions would not be honoured – that he put into this text 'a heart-rending sadness in which we can sometimes even sense a tone of despair'. If Francis recalls there his reverence for the churches and his faith in the priests, including the theologians, he also evokes the crucial role of lepers in his conversion, the inspiration that he received from God alone to define his ideal: the duty of manual labour, the necessity to stay 'only as a stranger and pilgrim' in poor churches and convents, the absolute prohibition on asking for favours from the Roman court, and the strict duty to follow the Rule and the *Testament* without adding anything or taking anything away, and without putting glosses on them.

Finally, in the 'Short Testament', which Saint Francis dictated to Brother Benedict in April 1226, after blessing 'all my brothers who are in the Order and who will enter it until the end of the world' ('tutti i miei frati i quali sono nell'Ordine e che vi entreranno fino alla fine del mondo'), he reiterates the three core principles: love among all the brothers of the Order, respect for 'Our Lady Sacred Poverty' ('nostra signora la Santa Povertà'), and obedience to the 'Holy Mother Church' ('Santa madre Chiesa').

That which remains of the letters, even if restricted to those that are definitely authentic, is testimony to Francis's epistolary activity among his close associates, the Order and all Christians. Of his letters to friends, one to Brother Leo survives.

> I am telling you, my son, like a mother, everything that we have said on the road in a few words and one piece of advice; and you do not need to come to me later for counsel, because here is what I advise, 'In whatever way seems best to

you to please God and to follow his footsteps and poverty, do it with the blessings of God and with my obedience. But if you need this for your soul and for your consolation and if you want to come to me, Leo, then come.'[10]

It was for Brother Leo again that he intended an exceptional document, an autograph parchment by Francis conserved in the Sacro Convento of Assisi, bearing on one side 'The Praises of God', and on the other 'A Blessing for Brother Leo' with the sign of the tau – Francis wrote it in September 1224, on La Verna. Another friendly letter is the one he had sent shortly before his death, asking her to hurry if she wanted to see him still alive, to the only female figure besides Saint Clare who appears in his life – the noble Roman lady Giacoma di Settesoli, whom he called 'frate Giacomina' and who prepared an almond cake for him that he took pleasure in eating when he was ill in Rome.

Letters concerning the Order's activities include a letter of obedience in which he ordered Brother Agnello of Pisa to go to England to fulfil the office of minister there, a letter to a minister speaking to him of problems concerning the Rule that he had to consider before the Pentecost chapter, and a letter to the general chapter and all the brothers. The last letter contained, besides his confession for having sinned 'either through negligence, or because of my weakness, or because I am ignorant and uneducated' ('sia per negligenza, sia a cagione della mia infermità, sia perchè sono ignorante e illetterato'), prescriptions concerning the Eucharist, Mass, Holy Scripture and singing (in which one must concentrate not 'on the melody of the voice but on identifying with the spirit' 'alla melodia della voce ma alla rispondenza della mente').

The correspondence to Christendom comprises a letter to all the clergy and one to all the faithful. The first, whose text comes from the monastery of Subiaco (with which Saint Francis maintained relations as much due to his taste for eremitism as to his desire to be attached to an authentic Benedictine tradition), called upon the clergy to respect the Holy Sacrament. The second, which was rather long, was a call to penance. The striking image that is made there of the impenitent man, dying among his relatives and friends, who were pretending to cry and eager to get their hands on his fortune, reveals both the satirical talent of the saint and the appearance of a theme that was to become very popular at the end of the Middle Ages.

The hymns and prayers are no less revealing of an even more profound aspect of the genius of the saint: his poetic and lyrical sensibility. 'The Praises of God', 'A Salutation of Virtues', 'A Salutation of the Blessed Virgin Mary', and 'The Office of the Passion of Our Lord' bear witness to Francis's liturgical sense, to his need to complete his meditation and contemplation with effusive outbursts, and to the focuses of his devotion. These were the Lord as almighty Creator, Christ the Crucified, the Virgin as the Lady of the Lord, 'his palace, his servant and his mother', and the virtues as the Holy Ladies of religion: holy Wisdom, pure and holy Simplicity, holy Poverty, holy Humility, holy Charity and holy Obedience. But this contribution of Saint Francis to spiritual poetry, so characteristic of the thirteenth century, is eclipsed by his lyrical masterpiece, 'The Canticle of the Creatures'. Renan called this poem, which gives Italian poetry a marvel for its beginning, 'the most beautiful piece of religious poetry since the Gospels'. It sums up all of Francis's brotherly love for all creation. Having spread everywhere his love for living creatures, people and animals, he sings his love for inanimate creatures to which he gives life and soul, all the way to 'our sister death'. He had the song sung to him at the Portiuncula by Brother Angelo and Brother Leo when he felt death approaching.

Saint Francis: medieval or modern?

The novelty of the message of Francis, the novelty of his way of life and his apostolate, first struck his own contemporaries. It might be thought that Thomas of Celano, who tended to insist on the originality of the saint whose disciple he was, and of the Order to which he belonged and for whose publicity he was, to some degree, responsible, could have exaggerated this factor. However, it should be borne in mind that in an era when tradition was an essential value and when any novelty was shocking, he must have had a strong motivation to emphasise the novelty of Francis and his work:

> In a time when evangelical doctrine was sterile, not only in his country but in the whole universe, he was sent by God to bear witness throughout the entire world, like the Apostles, to the truth. He proved with evidence by his teachings that all the wisdom of the world is but folly and in a short time, guided

by Christ, he brought people back to the true wisdom of God. The *new* evangelist of our age spread throughout the world, like a river of Paradise, the living waters of the Gospel and preached by his example the way of the son of God and the doctrine of truth. In him and by him the world experienced an unexpected revival and a re-*new*al of sanctity [*sancta novitas*]; the fertilisation of the antique religion soon *renewed* a world that had become old in routine and in tradition. A *new* spirit was inspired in the hearts of the elected, and the anointing of salvation was spread among them, when, like a star, the servant and saint of Christ illuminated them with a *new* rite and *new* signs. Through him the ancient miracles were *renewed*, and in the desert of this world, following an antique tradition but through a *new* order, a fertile vine was planted.*

(*Vita prima*, 89)

The historians of the late nineteenth and the twentieth centuries echoed and exalted the *modernity* of Saint Francis as the initiator of the Renaissance and the modern world. The Frenchman Émile Gebhart, in *L'Italie mystique* (Paris, 1906), associated Francis of Assisi with Frederick II and saw in these first two great *moderns* of the Middle Ages those who – each in his own sphere – had liberated Italy and Christendom from contempt for the world, obsession with the Devil, and the burden of the Antichrist. Francis was the *liberator*,

The distinctive features of the Franciscan religion, freedom of spirit, love, pity, joyful serenity and familiarity were long to form the originality of Italian Christianity, so different from the Pharisaic faith of the Byzantines, the fanaticism of the Spanish, and the scholastic dogmatism of Germany and France. There was none of that which, everywhere else, darkened or diminished consciousness; no subtle metaphysics, no refined theology, no casuistic concerns, no excesses of discipline and penance, and no extreme scrupulousness of devotion were henceforth to burden the Italians.

* Where, as here, words in quotations from St Francis or the biographers are in italics, these have been inserted by the author of this book to emphasise a particular point.

There is an area for which it has been claimed that the influence of Saint Francis, his sensibility and his devotion, were decisive and engaged the West on new pathways in modernism – art. The shock of Franciscanism is thus placed at the origin of the Renaissance. The German Henry Thode argued this in 1885 in an epoch-making book, *Franz von Assisi und die Anfänge der Kunst des Renaissance in Italien* ('Francis of Assisi and the Beginnings of Renaissance Art in Italy'). Francis, he claims, dramatised the Christian religion and played a crucial role in the development of the *lodi* and the *sacre rappresentazioni*. He also popularised the taste for moralising anecdotes, the *exempla*; hence the references in painting to anecdotes and contemporary life. He discovered nature in its palpable form and introduced the portrait and the landscape into iconography. Realism and narrative in art, according to this theory, come from him.

But a more attentive examination has revealed that most of the currents whose origins were attributed to Saint Francis had earlier sources. An examination of specific themes shows how, at the turn of the twelfth to thirteenth century, the image of Christ in glory on painted crucifixes changes to that of Christ in pain, the Virgin in majesty declined in favour of the Virgin of maternity, and the iconography of the saints tended less to stereotyped figures and symbolic attributes and more towards true biography and accurate features.

As early as 1215, the Paliotto de Berardenga at the Pinacoteca of Siena narrates the story of the Passion on six little panels, with an episode on each, around an enthroned Christ. Similarly, historians have been struck by the novelty of the type of saint Francis imposed on his contemporaries. This is to be found as early as Thomas of Celano's *Vita prima*, where, next to the description of the inner personality of Francis, his outer physique is described, with very precise and detailed realism: that is, a Francis whose bodily appearance contrasts with the traditional beauty of the tall, blond saint – an aesthetic canon borrowed from the Nordic knight.

Francis is described there as follows:

> of medium height, almost short, with a round, medium-sized head, a long face, a small, flat forehead, medium-sized eyes, black and naive, very dark hair, straight eyebrows, a small and rectilinear nose, straight but small ears, flat temples, well-aligned teeth, regular and white, thin lips, a black beard,

uneven hair, a thin neck, straight shoulders, short arms, small hands, tapering fingers, long fingernails, thin legs, smooth skin, a lank body.

The only contemporary portrait of Francis, that of Subiaco (see Plate 11), painted more the inner person, according to the canons of traditional beauty,[11] while the later one of Greccio (see Plate 12) indeed conjures up the dark little man who must have spoken to charm the crowds, the 'little black hen' to which he compared himself. This Francis of poor appearance is the same one found in the *Fioretti*, begging unsuccessfully with Brother Masseo,

> Saint Francis looked like a man who was too contemptible and short in height, and anyone who did not know him took him for a lowly little pauper, and so he gleaned only a few mouthfuls and scraps of dry bread. But to Brother Masseo, because he was a tall and handsome figure of a man, people gave lots of big, choice morsels and entire loaves.

But this realistic portrait of a saint had already been generally sketched more than a half century earlier in the *Vita* of Saint Bernard where the outer man, without being the object of so much attention as the inner man, is nevertheless described without complaisance.

For the rest, Francis was indeed in harmony with the main tendencies of Gothic sensibility, concerned with realism, with light, with delicacy. But if he did not create this sensibility, through his reputation and influence that continued in his Order, he supported and strengthened it to a remarkable degree. In 'The Canticle of the Creatures', despite an allusion to the symbolism of the sun, an image of God, it is in their tangible being and their physical beauty that the stars, the wind, the clouds, the sky, fire, flowers and grass are first seen and loved. The love that he bore for them was transmitted to those artists who, from then on, wanted to represent them *faithfully*, without distorting them or burdening them with the weight of alienating symbols. He did the same for animals, who from being symbolic became real.

Thus if Saint Francis was modern, it is because his century was so. And it does not diminish either his originality or his significance to observe, as Luigi Salvatorelli has admirably done, that 'he did not emerge like a magic tree in the middle of the desert', but that he was the product of a place and time, 'communal Italy at its peak'.

In this context, three phenomena are decisive for the orientation of Francis: class struggle, the rise of the laity, and the advance of the money economy.

He was struck very early on by the bitterness and frequency of the social and political struggles in which he must have taken part himself before his conversion. The struggles between the partisans of the Pope and the partisans of the Emperor, between cities and between families only increased and aggravated the oppositions between social groups. Francis who, as the son of a merchant, was between the popular strata and the nobility, belonging to the people by birth but close to the aristocracy by fortune, culture and way of life, was especially sensitive to these divisions. He always wanted to be humble towards his superiors, but also towards his equals and his inferiors. Thus, he received the warning of a peasant working in his field, which Francis was crossing on a donkey: he urged him not to disappoint the faith that many put in him and to be as good as people said he was. Francis got off his donkey, kissed the peasant's feet and thanked him for his advice.

By contrast, he guessed the thoughts of Brother Leonard who was walking alongside him as he rode a donkey and who was saying to himself: 'His parents and mine did not play together as equals. And here he is riding while I am on foot and leading his donkey.' Francis at once got off his donkey and said, 'My brother, it is not right that I should ride and you should walk because in the world you were more noble and powerful than I.' It was indeed his aim to overcome these social divisions by making his Order an example of equality, and in his human contacts setting the example of descending to the lowest level, that of the poor, the sick and beggars. And, inside secular society, he sought to bring back peace, to be a peacemaker. To the Perugians, always ready to assault their neighbours, he predicted that internal quarrels would tear them apart and that by this judgment of God they would be forced in a bloodstained manner to rediscover the supreme good, harmony, *unitas*. Similarly, Thomas of Spalato, who witnessed him preaching in Bologna on 15 August 1222, described the scene as follows:

> His speech had nothing of the tone or manners of a preacher; it
> was more like a conversation and aimed only to calm hatred

and restore peace. The clothing of the orator was miserable, his appearance wretched, and his face without beauty; but for all that his speech succeeded in reconciling the Bolognese nobles who for generations had not stopped spilling one another's blood.[12]

In any house he entered, he began by saying, 'Peace on this house', and in his letter to all the faithful he started by wishing them 'true peace'.

But how to restore this peace? First, lay people had to be associated in the life of the Church instead of being subject to the domination of the clergy and liable to excommunications and prohibitions (like the one Innocent III imposed on Assisi in 1204), which lost any effectiveness through being misused. Francis wanted his brothers to form not the Order that was in fact imposed on him, but a fraternity, a confraternity in which clergy and laity would cohabit. Thus he willingly accepted the institution of the Third Order. As much as to the clergy, he addressed his words to the nobles who had fashioned a culture, the knightly culture, the merchants who had started to dominate the cities, and the humble people who showed, by their work or their revolt, their role in society. In the finale of the Rule of 1221, he listed them beside the clergy:

all the big children and the little children, rich and poor, kings and princes, workers and farmers, serfs and masters, to all the virgins, continent or married, to the laity, men and women, to all the babies, the adolescents, young and old, healthy and sick, to all the humble and the great and to all the people, families, tribes and languages, to all the nations and to all the people everywhere on earth.

It was thus necessary to preach, to preach the Gospel, to all the people. But what was essential in the Gospel? What was being forgotten and compromised all around him? It was simplicity and poverty. The progress of agriculture and the sales of the resulting surpluses, together with the expansion of small and big businesses: these were spreading corruption at an ever faster rate through the increasing attraction of the money that was replacing the simple practices of autarky and bartering. The way to salvation had been shown by Christ in the Gospel of St Matthew, as Francis had heard it at the Portiuncula. 'If you want to be perfect, go, sell all that you own and give it to the poor and you will have treasure in Heaven; come, follow me.' To this was added another renunciation: 'He who would leave his father and his mother, his brothers and his sisters, his wife and his children, his houses and his fields for love of me, he will receive a hundredfold and will possess eternal life.' Giving up money was linked with giving up the family, a consequence of the gospel and Francis's troubles with his own family, and an element of the social and psychological context in which he was living. Indeed, at the beginning of the thirteenth century, the traditional family institution had been disrupted. A gap had opened up between the extended family of noble lineage or of the (willingly) docile peasant community and the nuclear family made up of direct ascendants and descendants only, which had not yet come into being

But in what way was Francis's response to the questions of the day a modern one?

He brought the knightly culture and sensibility that he had acquired before his conversion into his new religious ideal: Poverty was his Lady, Lady Poverty; the Holy Virtues were so many courtly heroines; the saint was God's knight understudied by a troubadour, a jongleur. The chapters of the Portiuncula were inspired by the gatherings at the Round Table around Arthur. Does Saint Francis's modernity then amount to introducing the ideal of chivalry into Christianity, just as the early Christians had introduced the ancient ideal of sport – the holy athlete of Christ – and Saint Bernard the military ideal of the first chivalry – the *Militia of Christ*?

Francis's strictly religious orientations may seem just as traditional. The hermit tradition goes back at least to the establishment of Christianity in the fourth century and has continued uninterruptedly ever since. In all the hermitages that Francis and his companions stayed in, they were no different, at first glance, from a whole range of hermits who, at that time, haunted the caves, the forests and the heights all over Italy, from Calabria to the north of the Apennines. Manual labour is connected as much with original Benedictine practice as with the monastic reform of the eleventh–twelfth centuries led by Prémontré or Cîteaux. From the end of the eleventh century, poverty was the motto of all these *Pauperes Christi*, these 'Paupers of Christ' who were swarming all over Christendom.

Was Francis's originality merely that he resisted the temptation of heresy to which most of these Paupers had ceded? Certainly, back in the early thirteenth century, some of them managed to remain within the Church: in 1201 a community of orthodox Humiliates, in 1208 the *Poveri Cattolici* of the Waldensians converted by Durando di Huesca and in 1210 another group of Waldensians around Bernardo Primo. But these were far outnumbered by the crowd of Albigensians and in Italy itself, in Francis's time, the Cathars who had a bishop in Florence and a school at Poggibonsi, and the Patarins, the Arnaldists, and the Waldensians. In 1218, a congress of *Poveri Lombardi* took place in Bergamo; in 1215, Milan was called a 'pit of heretics' (*fossa di eretici*); in 1227 Florence was still considered to be infested with heresy.

And, first of all, did Francis really almost become a heretic himself? The tendencies and the circumstances need to be analysed. There were certainly elements in both that could have led Francis to heresy. The uncompromising will to practise an integral Gospel, divested of all the contributions of the later history of the Church, the distrust of the Roman curia, the will to have almost absolute equality reign between the Minors and to allow for the duty of disobedience, the passion for simplicity taken to the extreme of nudism that Francis and his brothers practised, following the example of the Adamatists, the position granted to the laity – all this seemed dangerous, almost suspect, to the Roman curia. And, joining its efforts to those of the ministers and custodians who had been frightened to find so much intransigence in Francis, it put pressure on him and demanded of him, if not denials, at least renunciations that certainly led him to the brink of heretical temptation in 1223. He resisted it. Why? Very probably, in the first place, because he never entertained the feelings that led one part of the Franciscan Spirituals to heresy at a later date. Francis was neither a millenarian nor an apocalyptic. He never interposed an eternal Gospel, a mythical Golden Age, between the earthly world where he was living and the hereafter of Christianity. He was not the angel of the sixth seal of the Apocalypse with which he was unduly identified by certain Spirituals. The heretical eschatological lucubrations of the Spirituals came from Joachim of Fiore, not from Francis.

But what restrained him especially was the basic determination, endlessly repeated when he was not under pressure, for him and his brothers to remain at all costs (and he did pay dearly for it) within the Church. Why? Probably because he did not want to break the unity, or better, the community that he valued so much. But above all because of his feeling, of his visceral need, for the sacraments. Almost all the medieval heresies were opposed to the sacraments. Now, in his deepest being, Francis needed the sacraments and, to begin with, the first among them, the Eucharist. To deliver these sacraments, a clergy and a Church were necessary. Also, Francis – and this may be surprising – was ready to forgive the clergy a great deal in exchange for this ministry of the sacraments. In an epoch when even orthodox Catholics were questioning the validity of sacraments administered by unworthy priests, Francis recognised it and said so unreservedly. It was because he carefully distinguished the clergy from the laity that he needed the former and stayed within the Church.

Therefore it has been said of him that like Saint Dominic but in different ways, he saved the Church when it was threatened with ruination by heresy and its own internal decadence. He realised the dream of Innocent III. Some, furthermore, have found this shocking and deplorable. Machiavelli said,

> The power of their new orders is the reason why the improbity of the prelates and the heads of our religion does not ruin it; for still living in poverty and having great influence with the people because of hearing confessions and preaching, they give them to understand that it is evil to speak evil of what is evil, and that it is good to live under the prelates' control and, if prelates make errors, to leave them to God for punishment. So the prelates do the worst they can, because they do not fear that punishment which they do not see and do not believe in.[13]

It is true that Francis was one of these alibis that the Church, entrenched in the world, finds from time to time.

Francis, then, may now be perceived as orthodox and more traditional than has often been thought. Was he not really an innovator? The answer is yes, and on essential points.

In taking and in giving Christ himself, and no longer his apostles, as a model, he engaged Christianity in an imitation of the God-Man that restored the highest ambitions and an infinite horizon to the doctrine of love for humanity.

In resisting the temptation of solitude, going into the midst of living society, into the towns, and not to the deserts, the forests or the wilds, he broke decisively with a monasticism of separation.

By proposing as a programme a positive ideal, open to love for all creatures and all creation, rooted in *joy* and not in morose *accedia*, in sadness, and by refusing to be the ideal monk of the tradition dedicated to *tears*, he revolutionised the medieval and Christian sensibility and rediscovered a basic joyfulness, which was quickly smothered by a masochistic form of Christianity.

In making Christian spirituality part of the secular chivalrous culture of the troubadours and the lay popular culture of peasant folklore with its animals and its natural universe, the wonderful Franciscan lifted the lid that clerical culture had closed tightly upon the old traditional culture of humanity.

This return to the sources was also the sign and pledge of renewal and progress. The term 'return to the sources' recalls that in the last resort Franciscanism was *reactionary*. In the context of thirteenth-century modernity, the reaction of Francis was not that of a social misfit like Joachim or Dante, but of a man who wanted to preserve essential values in the face of change. Some of these reactionary tendencies could appear empty and even dangerous: in the century of universities, he rejected learning and books; in the century when the first ducats, the first florins, the first gold crowns were struck, he had a visceral hatred of money. In the Rule of 1221, in defiance of any economic sense, Francis cried out, 'We must not grant more usefulness to money and to coins than to pebbles.'[14] Is this not dangerous and foolish? It would be if Francis had wanted to extend his Rule to all humanity. But in fact Francis did not even want to transform his companions into an Order, but only wanted to gather together a little group, an elite that would provide a counterweight, a question mark, an eddy in the rising tide of material comfort. This counterweight of Franciscanism has continued to be needed in the modern world, by believers and non-believers alike. And since Francis, in his words and by his example, preached it with a burning intensity, a purity and a poetry that are unsurpassable, Franciscanism still remains today, in the words of Thomas of Celano, a 'sancta novitas', a sacred innovation. The Poverello is not only one of the protagonists of history, but one of the guides of humanity.

The Canticle of the Creatures or The Song of Brother Sun

Most High, all-powerful and good Lord
yours are the praises, glory, honour and every blessing

to you alone, Most High, they do belong
and no one is worthy to speak your name.
Praised be you, my Lord, with all your creatures
especially Sir Brother Sun
through whom you give us the day and light
he is beautiful, radiant with great splendour,
and of you, Most High, he is our symbol.
Praised be you, my Lord, for Sister Moon and the Stars
in heaven you created them clear and precious and beautiful.
Praised be you, my Lord, for Brother Wind,
and for the air, and for the clouds
for the calm blue skies and for every changing weather
through them, you sustain life in all your creatures.
Praised be you, my Lord, for Sister Water
who is very useful and humble
precious and chaste.
Praised be you, my Lord, for Brother Fire
through whom you light up the night,
he is beautiful and joyful,
wild and strong.
Praised be you, my Lord, for our Sister, Mother Earth
who bears and nourishes us
who produces the many different fruits
and the colourful flowers and herbs.
Praised be you, my Lord, for those
who grant forgiveness for the love of you,
who endure trials and illness,
Blessed are they who endure in peace
for by you, Most High, they will be crowned.
Praised be you, my Lord, for our Sister Bodily Death
from whom no one living can escape,
woe to those who die in mortal sin,
blessed are they she finds doing Your will
because the second death cannot harm them.
Praise and bless my Lord,
and give Him thanks and serve Him
with all humility.

THE VOCABULARY OF SOCIAL CATEGORIES IN SAINT FRANCIS OF ASSISI AND HIS THIRTEENTH-CENTURY BIOGRAPHERS

The problems of historiography posed, on the one hand, by the authenticity of some of the writings of Saint Francis and, on the other, by the objectivity of some of the testimonies of his first biographers are assumed to be known in their general outlines.[1] These problems are simply mentioned below in so far as this traditional textual criticism affects our research. Here again, we must work on two levels, relating the vocabulary of our texts to what we know from elsewhere of the realities that it designates, and relating this vocabulary to the mental world of its users.

The texts to be considered are contained in the slim volume of Saint Francis's complete works,[2] that is, the two Rules, the *Testament*, the letters, the prayers and the liturgical texts, and in the biographies assembled by the Fathers of Quaracchi.[3] Among these latter works, we have mainly used those of the following authors:

1   Thomas of Celano, an Italian Franciscan born in the Abruzzi Mountains, lived for part of his life in Germany, but mostly in Italy, and joined the Order towards 1215 'with many other educated and noble men' ('cum pluribus aliis viris litteratis et nobilibus'). The works used include:

This chapter was first published as a paper in *Ordres et classes. Colloque d'histoire sociale, Saint-Cloud, 24–25 mai 1967*, Paris and The Hague, Mouton, 1973, pp. 93–103.

- the *Vita prima*, written in 1228 at the request of Pope Gregory IX;
- the *Legenda chori* (1230);
- the *Vita secunda* (1246–47);
- the *Tractatus de miraculis* (1250–2).

2 Julian of Speyer, a German Franciscan, lived mostly in Paris where he studied the liberal arts, particularly music ('before he entered the Order he had been master of singing at the court of the king of France and was remarkable for his learning and holiness', 'ante Ordinis ingressum fuit magister cantus in aula regis Francorum, scientia et sanctitate conspicuus'). He entered the Order before 1227 and taught music in the Convent of Saint Jacques in Paris. The works used include:

- a *Vita* (of around 1232–5), very close to Thomas of Celano's *Vita prima*;
- an *Officium rhythmicum* (around 1231–2).

3 Henri d'Avranches was a secular 'travelling cleric who carried out missions for kings' ('clericus vagus et pro regibus legationibus fungens') at the court of England, the court of Frederick II in Germany, and the pontifical court. He was known as '*magister Henricus versificator*': his *Legenda versificata*, written on the basis of Thomas of Celano's *Vita prima*, at the request of Gregory IX (around 1232–4) has been used.

4 Saint Bonaventure, an Italian Franciscan, was born into a family of burghers (father a small town doctor), and studied in Paris, where he occupied one of the two chairs of theology of the Order at the University. He then became master general of the Order in 1257: his *Legenda major* and *Legenda minor* have been used, both written at the request of the general chapter of Narbonne in 1260 to be 'official lives' to replace those written previously (which were ordered to be destroyed) and presented to the general chapter of Pisa in 1263.

5 Jacobus de Voragine, an Italian Dominican, was prior of Lombardy and then archbishop of Genoa: his 'Vita S. Francisci' in the *Golden Legend* (written between 1265 and 1280), has been used, which draws on the *Vita secunda* and *The Treatise on the Miracles* by Thomas of Celano and the *Legenda major* by Saint Bonaventure.

6 An anonymous German Benedictine of the Oberaltaich convent in Bavaria wrote *Legenda monacensis*. This *Vita*, known as 'The Legend of Munich', of *ca.* 1275 is based on the two *Vitae* of Thomas of Celano and Saint Bonaventure, and has been used.

Definition and scope of the research

Its significance

Franciscanism was a great religious movement that, more than any other Mendicant Order, awakened, influenced and pervaded the whole of Christian society in the thirteenth century, the century of its birth. It used new methods of apostleship. Breaking with the isolation of earlier monasticism, it sent its members onto the roads, and especially into the towns, at that time growing rapidly,[4] into the very heart of society. Its success was brilliant in every milieu. Saint Francis of Assisi, its founder, with his historic and legendary personality, was mainly responsible for this success. His works and those of his first biographers comprise the main arsenal on which the Franciscans drew to act upon the society of their time, by words and by example. What, then, does this arsenal teach us about that society?

Three qualities endow this set of texts with an exemplary value in this respect.

The basis of their effectiveness rests on a certain analysis of the global society. Of course, the Franciscans' implements were used with the object of transforming society, not describing it. Moreover, any vocabulary or any language is not only an instrument of analysis and of understanding but also an attitude and an instrument of action. But, in the high Middle Ages, the cultural passivity of the mass of society (rooted in the social and political subjection that left it little more than heresy as an expression of revolt) made it possible for the Church to act upon society by means of a 'terrorist' language of the sacred (use of Latin, idealist symbolism, lack of realism in Romanesque art, etc.). The emancipation of an increasing number of categories in secular society (the nobility, urban strata, *rustici* less rigidly defined and supported by heretical organisations) made this language increasingly inoperative. The Franciscans' concern to be effective in the new society demanded a language, a vocabulary, with a certain relationship with reality, and primarily with social reality, in its group institutions.

At the same time, the concern of Saint Francis and his disciples to address the whole of society ('all the people, all created beings', 'omnes homines, omnes creaturae') led them to use systems of denomination covering *all* the social categories.

The set of texts has a sufficient homogeneity because of the following:

- the fact that all these texts revolve around one man, his experience and his teachings: Saint Francis;
- the predominance, among these authors, of a group modelled by the same training and the same ideal: the Franciscans; this family resemblance is reinforced by the influence of one biographer on almost all the others: Thomas of Celano;
- the fact that most, or at least the most important, of their actual experiences took place in the same geographical location: central and northern Italy;
- the fact that all these authors belonged, if not to the same generation, at least to the same period, between about 1220 and 1280, and essentially 1220–63 – a period it would be tempting to call 'the thirteenth century of Saint Louis', but this would take us outside Italy.

However, the set of texts also has enough diversity to make variations possible.

From the viewpoint of chronology

If this 'beautiful thirteenth century' was a period when new institutions were established and a new equilibrium was achieved, it was also a time 'when history accelerated' – which makes it possible to test the faculty of resistance or adaptation of the structures of language and mental attitudes. From a narrower perspective, during this period the Franciscan Order experienced a development whose impact on its vocabulary must be measured.

From the viewpoint of the authors

Despite the uniformity of the Franciscan mould, the differences in the social and geographical origins of the authors, in their training (and particularly whether or not they had been through university), and in their careers and personalities create a diversity, which is intensified by the presence among them of a Dominican, a Benedictine and a member of the laity.

From the viewpoint of literary genres

Although hagiographical conventions (which were, in any case, changing, Saint Francis himself being both a main reflection of and factor in this development[5]) are predominant, the diversity of the genres can indicate how resistant they were to the same influence. In the case of Saint Francis, the range was according to the more or less 'official' nature of his writings, from the Rule to the letters. In the case of the biographers, the indication lay between the genres more open to novelty (prose biography of the *Vita* or *Legenda* type) and those more locked into a formal tradition (written in verse, or in a liturgical style). This raises the question of whether the more 'traditional' and even reactionary character of the terms and themes in Henri d'Avranches was not due as much to the 'system' of scholarly poetry in the first half of the thirteenth century as it was to his situation as a secular individual connected to court circles.[6]

But, however favourable this series of texts seems to be to the study of the relationships between the social vocabulary appearing in it and what we can define, in current scholarly terms, as the social reality of the times, it nonetheless displays a series of characteristics that not only acts as a screen between the language and the social structure, but also highlights the difficulties that the historian, and particularly the medievalist, encounters in the scholarly use of the vocabulary of the past.

Its difficulties

Difficulties inherent in medieval literature

THE LANGUAGE

The language of all our texts is Latin. However, far from simplifying the study of vocabulary, this apparent uniformity poses major problems, two in particular. Since in the Middle Ages Latin was both a dead and a living language, to what contemporary realities did the words refer?

What approximations, distortions, counter-meanings and puns came into play between the words and their ancient and medieval meanings (for example *dux, miles*, etc.)? Significantly, the pressure of the vernacular language on culture increased greatly in the thirteenth century; what relationships did the literary Latin vocabulary maintain with the vocabulary in the vernacular language? In the case of a new type of apostolate, like that of Saint Francis, do these Latin–vernacular relationships not pose special problems?[7]

THE RELIGIOUS 'WELTANSCHAUUNG'

Religions, and particularly universal religions like Christianity, tend to combat class struggle by denying it. This denial 'dissocialises' the superstructures, specifically art and literature, letting 'social realism' slip in only surreptitiously. The religious schemas of society are different from the actual social structures. Sometimes – this is the Dionysian model[8] – the human hierarchy is traced on the celestial hierarchy which, furthermore, is often merely a more or less unconscious transposition of a given historical social structure.[9] Sometimes inequalities were founded on properly religious criteria (for example in relation to sin, which led medieval theologians to make curious assimilations between the *servus peccati* and the simple *servus*), and distinctions between groups were founded on liturgical or mystical criteria enshrining a hierarchy of genders (men, women) or family situations (virginity, widowhood, marriage). Above all, the split between the clergy and the laity was fundamental.

Even though Franciscanism sought to bring the apostolate closer to real social conditions, and sometimes indeed by virtue of its desire to transform terrestrial society into a society of salvation (a tendency obviously more pronounced among the 'Joachimite' Franciscans, but true of all of them), it maintained a deliberate conceptual and verbal confusion towards social categories.[10]

BIBLICAL BORROWINGS

All language is in part a heritage. However, in the Middle Ages, this heritage was particularly constraining; the Book contained all knowledge, language included, and language primarily. The Bible was the arsenal of vocabulary and of mental models. For words as for everything

else, any innovation was suspect. Doubtless, the Bible lends itself to all
sorts of interpretations, and it is so rich and diverse that we can find in it
almost anything that we looking for. As Alain de Lille put it, biblical
citations have a 'nose of wax'.[11] Indeed, at the beginning of the
thirteenth century, authority in the literal sense – quotation – no
longer constituted the whole of a demonstration or reasoning: dialectics
and scholastics were teaching the clerics to fly with their own wings.

But if from the point of view of language Francis of Assisi and
Franciscanism represented progress towards vernacular speech, and if
from the ideological point of view they sought to compromise between
the desire for an inclusive vocabulary and the tendency to establish a
religious society immediately, from the point of view of the use of the
Bible they were distinctly 'reactionary'.

For them the Gospel was the foundation of everything. Certainly,
Thomas of Celano defines Saint Francis as a 'homo novus' and Francis-
canism as a 'sancta novitas', but this 'novelty' can be defined as the
Gospel, nothing but the Gospel, and the whole Gospel.

The Gospels were foregrounded over the rest of the Bible. For Saint
Francis, the great source was not the Old Testament but the New.
Out of 196 biblical quotations in the writings of Saint Francis, there
are only thirty-two from the Old Testament (of which nine are from
Psalms) and 164 from the New Testament (of which 115 are from the
four Gospels). The other authorities cited are Saint Jerome (once) and
Saint Augustine (once).[12]

To take stock of the importance of this real 'evangelical turn' in the
use of language, it should be recalled that the authors of the high Middle
Ages – this has been specifically studied in the case of Alcuin[13] –
borrowed the essentials of their political and social vocabulary from
the Old Testament. Now, the language of the Old Testament, though
more ceremonial, is also often more realistic. That of the New Testament, if it is more spiritual, is less realistic, even in the narrative
passages, in so far as it is intended specifically to transform, and sometimes to purge, the institutions and the spirit of the old law. Grace influences vocabulary by erasing and sublimating social categories. Now
Saint Francis, in his deep intentions and as seen by his biographers,
is, by any definition, a new apostle, a new evangelist and even a new
Jesus. Thus in the texts that we are studying, he meets more people
of the Gospels than people of his own time.

We must nevertheless concede that behind the evangelical vocabulary there were contemporary realities, and the effectiveness of the Franciscans is explicable only if this vocabulary was not only magical, but also resonant with the objective structures of the society that they addressed.

In addition, the vocabulary in the biographical writings on Saint Francis is less dependent on the Gospels than is the vocabulary of his own writings. For example, the two most frequently used words of their social vocabulary, *nobilis* and *miles*, scarcely appear in the Gospels; and while for the Franciscans, *miles* usually had the contemporary sense of knight, it of course had only the meaning of *soldier* for the evangelists. In passing, an example can be given of the mental contaminations that semantic change must have produced in the minds of the clerics of the Middle Ages, when the former sense bled into the new meaning. The *milites* of the Gospels hardly ever appear except in the episodes of the Passion. They are in the front line of Christ's torturers. This must have fed the hostility that most clerics of the Middle Ages – even those from the military aristocracy and aware of the community of interests of the two dominant classes, the ecclesiastic and the secular – nurtured towards the *milites*. Debate between a cleric and a knight is also a commonplace of the literature of the time of Saint Francis.

Sometimes, the Gospels provided the Franciscans with a vocabulary such as to highlight social oppositions that had a particular meaning in contemporary society. For instance, the *populus–turba* distinction (for example, in Matt. 4:23–25) may have made it easier for the biographers of Saint Francis to define and express the distinction between the nondescript crowds that gathered around him in the towns and the new 'popular' formations whose existence and activity he had noted in the combat of the class struggle that he was trying to appease.[14]

Thus if there is some discrepancy between the vocabulary of the Bible and the vocabulary in everyday use at the beginning of the thirteenth century, and a discrepancy between this vocabulary and the social realities of the era, the imbalance thus produced in the language is offset by the need that Saint Francis himself felt to take from the Gospels the words that he required to be in tune with his time. And the very study of this subtle interplay in the use of biblical vocabulary informs us on the needs and the realities of the era. Disuse of one word, the popularity of another, false meanings and misinterpretations, the need for a neologism and the whole range of semantic shifts and distortions are valuable indications.

Difficulties inherent in the chosen texts

TEXTS BY SAINT FRANCIS

The authenticity of certain texts by Saint Francis – especially of certain letters – is doubtful.[15] It is regrettable for our purpose that, for example, the 'Letter to Rulers of the Peoples' is not above all suspicions, at least as far as the actual words of the text are concerned. Furthermore, in our view a systematic internal study of the vocabulary of the whole group of works attributed to Saint Francis could make it easier to approach the problems of authenticity.

Two of Saint Francis's most important texts were composed under external influences. The *Regula bullata* is a compromise between the text prepared by the saint and the changes demanded by certain of his companions and by the Roman curia. But here, a comparison with the text of the Rule composed by the saint is, on the very level of the vocabulary, illuminating.

On the other hand, the *Testament* is a text dictated by the saint under circumstances that, as some have believed, reveal the influence of 'extremist' associates.[16] Here again, although in a less convincing manner, a comparison with other texts, the Rules notably, should be informative.

TEXTS OF THE BIOGRAPHIES

All these texts are to differing degrees tributary to the treatises written by the oldest and most important of all, Thomas of Celano. Some of them include entire sentences which are word for word repetition. If these variations around one model, one source, can make possible fine comparative analyses, just as often they condemn these efforts to being merely exercises in hair splitting.

Significantly, the close kinship of all these texts excludes a whole Franciscan family, that of the tendency of the future 'Spirituals', whose first area of disagreement with the orthodox tendency was precisely the interpretation of the character of Saint Francis, the nature of his intentions, his spirituality, his activity and his work. Despite

71

the considerable problems of dating, authenticity and attribution involved, our texts should be compared with the conserved and published texts[17] from the group which is not represented here and which is connected with the 'three companions', the *tres socii*, of whom the most important was certainly Brother Leo. However, a preliminary glance at these texts confirms what could have been guessed: the 'Spiritual' tendency is, in its outlook, in its writings, and in its conceptual and verbal armoury, the most 'asocial', the least realistic, and the most hostile to the world. Like the Cathars – with whom they had in fact no direct ties – the Spirituals were in great haste to begin to purify the world while ignoring its social structures, for them, among the impure incarnations of its evil nature.

Elements of the vocabulary of social categories

In Saint Francis (according to his writings and his biographers)

The social vision of Saint Francis seems to be ordered around three societies: celestial society, terrestrial society composed of all Christian people, and the particular society comprising him and his brothers, for which he sought to define a role of favoured mediation between the two preceding societies.

Celestial society

If Saint Francis used the contemporary appellations of 'Lord' and 'King' to designate God, he did not develop the references to the feudal and monarchic hierarchies implied in the terms 'Dominus' and 'Rex'. In the enumeration of celestial society that is found in the first Rule,[18] he calls God 'king of heaven and earth' ('Rex coeli et terrae') and Christ 'Our Lord' ('Dominus noster'), but his list of the celestial hierarchy – from the Virgin, the archangels and angels to the saints – is free of any feudal or monarchic terminology, remaining content with properly religious and liturgical appellations. He seems a stranger to the Dionysian fashion of the time by which symmetry was established, on the feudal model, between celestial and terrestrial society. He does not seem to have made any correspondence between the two societies enumerated throughout the course of the first Rule. If celestial society

1

1 General view of Asssisi. At the meeting point of the plains and mountains, the compact urban area. To the left the cathedral, with alterations from the ninth to the thirteenth century (rededicated in 1228). To the right, the church of Santa Chiara (1257–65). The view is taken from the Basilica of Saint Francis – an insult to the saint's spirituality – which is not visible here.

2 *Solitude* (1). San Damiano. In this church, a solitary country oratory of the beginning of the thirteenth century, Saint Francis heard the crucifix speak to him in 1205.

3 *Solitude* (2). View of the Carceri, a hermitage on the slopes of Mount Subasio (at a height of 800 metres) and one hour's walk from Assisi, which the Benedictines gave Saint Francis. Saint Bernardino of Siena had a modest convent built there in the fifteenth century.

4 *The origins of Franciscan iconography*. Saint Francis with episodes of his life (Florence, Church of Santa Croce, Bardi chapel). This painting, from about 1240, an illustration of the first *Vita* of Thomas of Celano, contains the first figured representation, around the image of the saint, of the episodes then considered the most important in his life.

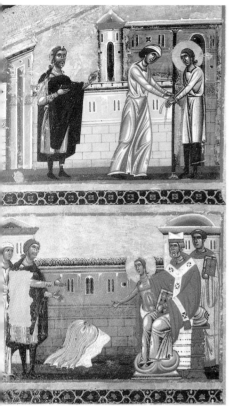

5   6

5 *Episodes of the life of Saint Francis*: liberation from prison in Perugia (above) and first renunciation of possessions (below). After the shocking experience of prison, Francis renounces his worldly goods and his father's business, between his parents, whom he is leaving, and the bishop, whom he is approaching, in his new nakedness. Florence, Santa Croce, Bardi chapel.

6 *Episodes of the life of Saint Francis*: approval of the Rule (above) and Christmas at Greccio (below). In the pontifical palace with its symbolic architecture, Francis, humbly kneeling, has the Pope accept the rule of the new Order. At Greccio, in nature symbolised by a stylised mountain and in the presence of a fraternal ox and donkey, Francis adores the baby Jesus, giving a great impetus to this worship. Florence, Santa Croce, Bardi chapel.

7 *Episodes of the life of Saint Francis. Sermon to the birds* (above): attentive and in good order on the ground, but still in disorder in the tree, the birds are an audience favoured by Francis. *Preaching to the Sultan* (below): Francis extends the basic Mendicant action of preaching to animals (celestial) and to Moslems (the word and the book replacing the sword and the crusade). Florence, Santa Croce, Bardi chapel.

9

10

8 *Episodes of the life of Saint Francis. The sailors' thanksgiving* (above): gratitude of the socially marginal. *A ship saved from shipwreck* (below): a great traditional miracle of Francis, who becalmed the sea. Florence, Santa Croce, Bardi chapel.

9 *Episodes of the life of Saint Francis. The stigmata* (above): a hermitage in a mountainous landscape and a seraph transmitting stigmata. *Extreme renunciation* (below): between his father and mother and their respective servants, Francis, near a column like that of Christ, renounces his clothing of a rich man's son. Florence, Santa Croce, Bardi chapel.

10 *Episodes of the life of Saint Francis. Caring for lepers and washing of feet* (above): the defining practice of works of compassion. *The apparition at Arles* (below): the resurrected Francis-Christ appears in heaven to his brothers, while Saint Anthony, an authentic companion who died in 1231, is delivering a sermon on the saint to the Arles chapter. Florence, Santa Croce, Bardi chapel.

11

11 The earliest portrait of Saint Francis. Fresco of the Master of San Gregorio (1228–9) in the Benedictine Sacro Speco of Subiaco, near Rome. Francis is not yet depicted with a saint's halo. Retouches to the fresco have transformed the short, dark man into a tall blond, to fit the stereotype of holiness.

12 *Saint Francis: the dark little man*. Portrait by Margheritone of Arezzo (second quarter of the thirteenth century). Vatican Museum.

12

13 Sermon to the birds. Affirmation of the tree and of nature. Assisi, lower Basilica, thirteenth century.

14 *Episodes of the life of Saint Francis.* Drawing by the Benedictine Matthew Paris, towards 1250, illustrating his *Chronica majora.* Evokes the sharp-beaked birds of Revelation. Cambridge, Corpus Christi College, manuscript 16.

15

16

15 *Giotto's gentler vision of Francis* (1). Saint Francis inside the church, restorer of orthodoxy. He is the incarnation of a dream of Pope Innocent III calling on the saint to rectify the leaning church. Giotto, Assisi, upper Basilica.

16 *Giotto's gentler vision of Francis* (2). Bucolic atmosphere of the sermon to the birds. Giotto, Assisi, upper Basilica.

obeys a hierarchical order, from God to the saints, there is no order in the enumeration of terrestrial society.[19]

If *Rex* was used relatively rarely to designate God, the word *Imperator* never appears in his writings, and in the biographies Saint Francis is made to call God 'the Great Emperor' only once ('Magnus Imperator': *Vita secunda*, 106, p. 193). Nor did Saint Francis ever mention an Emperor in terrestrial society, thereby refraining from giving it a *single* leader (an 'egalitarian' tendency, perhaps reinforced by a Guelphic stance?). In the story of his life, the only emperor mentioned is Otho IV who, in 1209, passed near Assisi, where Francis and his first brothers were staying. But Francis kept well away from the casual on-lookers who went to admire the imperial pomp and he forbade his brothers to join the crowds, apart from a single one of them who was made responsible for keeping up a constant chant reminding the Emperor that his glory would not endure.[20] Francis stated that the only thing he would have to say to the Emperor would be to have him pass an edict ordering all the owners of wheat and grain to scatter it in the streets so that the little birds 'and especially the sister larks' could take part in the festivities.[21] Of the kings and queens reigning in his lifetime, his biographers mention only Blanche of Castile and her son Saint Louis, the king and queen of France, a country for which Francis had a special predilection, on account of the special piety and notably the devotion to the Eucharist that he discerned in its sovereigns, both of whom were benefactors of the Minors from the very beginning and soon became associated with the spiritual and liturgical life of the Order.

But the title that Francis most readily granted to God was 'Pater', 'Father', since his ideal social model was a model family.[22] Similarly, although he once called the Virgin Mary 'Domina' and 'Regina', 'Lady' and 'Queen',[23] he generally saw her as the first among God's creatures, connected to the Holy Trinity by the closest family relation-ships, 'daughter' and 'servant' of the Father,[24] 'spouse' of the Holy Ghost,[25] and most important of course, 'mother' of Christ. But she is also the model of created beings, 'holy',[26] 'poor',[27] and 'gentle and beautiful'.[28]

Satan is the 'father of bad sons',[29] but he is never designated as the *prince* of darkness or of evil spirits, as if Francis wanted carefully to avoid anything that could resemble Manichaeism. He calls him very simply 'diabolus' or 'Satanas', while his biographers sometimes have recourse to the traditional circumlocutions 'ancient enemy' or 'old serpent'.

As far as the demons are concerned, the biographers indicate a revealing comparison. They were for Francis the 'gastaldi' of the Lord, the agents of his punishments. Francis added to this, maliciously, a reference to the courts of the great, of the 'magnati'.[30] This was a pessimistic conception of the power and of the agents of repression, connected not only to humanity's original sin, but also to the rebellion of the fallen angels. Without taking political pessimism as far as a Jean de Meung, Francis here initiated, as a theologian, a critique of power and of powers that we will see again.

Franciscan society

Saint Francis considered himself and his brothers from three points of view:

- *From a positive viewpoint:* at the time of their entry into the fraternity, they were seen neutrally but as a microcosm of terrestrial society since they came from two or three distinct social categories (that is, in the ecclesiastical schemas of the era). Among them were indeed at the same time: (1) the 'clergy' and the 'laity' (*clerici–laici*);[31] (2) the 'learned' and the 'ignorant' (*litterati–illiterati*);[32] (3) members of each of the three orders of the *tripartite society*, or rather, two of the orders of the tripartite society: 'those who pray' and 'those who work', *oratores* and *laboratores*, identified with the clergy and the laity.[33] But in the third category positive society is giving way to ideal society. If Francis excluded warriors, *bellatores*, from the third totality, it was probably not so much because he held a dualistic and dialectic concept of the totality (two opposites form a better whole than does a triad), but because he did not conceive that his Order could include warriors. This underscores his distance both from the traditional concept of monasticism formed of *milites Christi* (St Bernard's concept) as from the pattern, more modern at that time, of an *Ecclesia* with three aspects: *militans*, *laborans* and *triumphans*.[34]
- *From a normative viewpoint:* his Order (or his fraternity) brought together representatives of two groups of social and spiritual elites: the elite of 'all the inferiors' (the brothers were the supreme form

of *Minors*) – a particularly important perspective here because he enumerates the catalogue of undervalued social categories. He began by describing it: 'servus' (serf),[35] 'minister' (servant),[36] 'rusticus' (illiterate peasant),[37] 'mercenarius' (non-producer, economic dependant),[38] 'alpigena' (illiterate mountain dweller),[39] 'mercator' (merchant). Second he listed the categories that the Minors should emulate: 'the vile and despised people, the poor and weak, the sick, lepers, beggars and vagabonds' ('viles et despectas personas, pauperes et debiles, infirmos, leprosos, juxta viam mendicantes').[40] Among these, three categories seemed particularly 'commendable' to Francis: the 'unlettered' ('idiotae', an even more radical term than 'illiterati'), the 'obedient' ('subditi'), and above all the 'poor' ('pauperes').[41]

Two remarks are required here. First, Francis felt the need to specify who he meant by 'the poor', for fear that his brothers might understand it as the rather meaningless concept that so many clerics delighted in or repeated mechanically. The touchstone of socially real poverty was *begging*. Also Francis – after warning the brothers against the possession of that most accursed object, 'money' ('pecunia') – added that in case of necessity they must beg for it, 'sicut alii pauperes', 'like the other poor' – which certainly mean the *real* poor.[42] Second, the preference expressed by Francis for these three categories highlights what were for him the three great evils, the three main poles of repulsion of society: knowledge, power and wealth.

• *Finally, Francis encouraged his brothers to follow the model of another elite – the family.* His Order had to be in the first instance, in the literal sense, more of a *fraternity* or a *confraternity* of a secular type than an Order of a religious, ecclesiastical type to which he finally had to resign himself. Of these brothers, he would be the *father*, following the divine model, God being primarily for him, as we have seen, a Father.[43] But the kind of family he recommended to his brothers was quite strange. Their *fraternal* love had to be, in fact, of a *maternal* nature:[44] those who lived in hermitages had to divide themselves into pairs as *mother and son*, a distinction that also corresponded to that between Martha and Mary, between active and contemplative life.[45] To Brother Leo he spoke like a mother to a son.[46] Finally, in the letter to the faithful, when he gave himself up to the dream of a lay society that had become completely *spiritual*, after recalling the model of *serfdom* and *submission* ('servi et subditi'), he invoked a family ideal in which the faithful became the *spouses, brothers and mothers of Christ*, following a spiritual asceticism that was explicated in detail.[47]

This family reference appears all the more surprising as it does not seem to have any correspondence in the pre-religious life of Saint Francis. Here particularly, it is true, we have to rely on the biographers who, if they emphasise the conflict with the father at the moment of conversion and if they are not kind to the parents about Francis's upbringing, are thus merely conforming to the commonplaces of hagiography that dwell on the contrast between the life of the saint before and after his conversion and the breaking of the earthly bonds represented by the family. These common-places were vivified and reinforced by the christological model that dominated all the Franciscan biography. Here, like Christ, Francis also literally fulfilled the famous words of Matthew, chapter 10: 'Veni enim separare hominem adversus patrem suum, et filiam adversus matrem suam'. This passage, which was read by a priest at the Portiuncula at the end of 1208 or the beginning of 1209, played a crucial role in the conversion of Francis. Could these obscurities, these apparent contradictions to Francis's individual psychology, be clarified, perhaps with an analysis, indeed psychoanalysis, of the collective psychology of the original Franciscan group? With-out denying its potential significance, I do not recognise myself as capable of engaging in such research, in which errors would be only too easy to make. Let us remain content to observe that, for a Francis of Assisi, at the beginning of the thirteenth century, a family model of the narrow type constituted an ideal social schema.

Terrestrial Christian society

The apostolic message of Francis – this bears constant repetition – was addressed to everyone. Francis rooted this missionary concern in a profound need to embrace all of society, globally and individually.

On two occasions, he enumerated the components of this total society. In the 'Letter to the Faithful' he was content with a listing according to religious status, following the obvious division into regular clergy, secular clergy and laity (*religiosi, clerici, laici*), and according to gender ('men and women' – *masculi et feminae*), that he summarised and completed with the vague expression 'everybody who lives in the entire world' (*omnes qui habitant in universo mundo*).

In chapter twenty-three of the first Rule, he was much more explicit. He began with an enumeration of the religious world, in which he distinguished the 'ecclesiastical orders' (*ecclesiastici ordines*, namely *sacerdotes, diaconi, subdiaconi, acolythi, exorcistae, lectores, ostiarii*), completing the list by mentioning all the 'clerics' and 'monks', among whom he distinguished the 'religious', both male and female (*omnes clerici, universi religiosi et religiosae*). Passing on to secular society, he first named children, boys and girls (*omnes pueri, parvuli et parvulae*), then the 'poor' and 'indigent' (*pauperes et egeni*), 'kings' and 'princes' (*reges et principes*), 'labourers' and 'peasants' (*laboratores, agricolae*), 'serfs' and 'lords' (*servi et domini*), women, 'virgin, continent' or 'married' (*omnes virgines et continentes et maritatae*), the 'laity, male and female' (*laici, masculi et feminae*), 'children, adolescents, young and old' (*omnes infantes, adolescentes, iuvenes et senes*), 'healthy people' and the 'sick' (*sani et infirmi*), the 'small and the great' (*pusilli et magni*), and finally all the 'peoples, populations, tribes, linguistic groups, nations and all human beings everywhere on earth, present and future' (*et omnes populi, gentes, tribus et linguae, omnes nationes et omnes homines ubicumque terrarum, qui sunt et erunt*).[48]

Several of Saint Francis's major preoccupations can be recognised here. Among them are the concern for totality, which is discernible as much in the word choice ('omnes', 'universus', 'ubicumque') as in the overlap of the listed categories and the social, geographical and chronological scope; the deference to the priesthood and church society; and the attention to children, originating both from the evangelical and christological model and from the changing sensibility of the times. Another preoccupation is the priority given to the weak over the strong. The poor are mentioned before the kings. In the society of work, *laboratores* – which could mean either 'ploughmen', the rural elite or urban workers – *agricolae, servi* are mentioned before lords; the small come before the great. And his ultimate preoccupation is a missionary concern that embraces all the peoples of the globe.

It is more important for our purpose to make two remarks. First, Saint Francis mixes several schemas for describing society, following several criteria: religious status, age, gender, wealth, power, professional occupation and nationality. This is not merely a use of schemas familiar to

Christian ideology, concerned with the dismantling schemas of a socio-
professional type in such a way as to deny class division and struggle,
and better to make the weight of its ideological domination bear on a
society divided up according to its convenience.[49] Here what is mani-
fest above all is the desire to consider society as a set of categories
that are not hierarchic from a spiritual point of view and, with due
respect paid to church society, are all equal on the level of salvation
or, if anyone is favoured on that level, the advantage goes to the
unprivileged here below.

Second, Saint Francis preferred to use multiple or bipartite schemas
rather than the tripartite schemas which were then in fashion. Multiple
schemas seemed to him more concrete, closer to the real society that
was to be saved by knowing how to address it, as well as further from
the hierarchisation that he wanted nothing to do with. As for bipartite
schemas, they represented the type of earthly opposition that he wanted
to destroy through brotherhood, on the image of his fraternity that welcomed both the clergy and the laity, the literate and the illiterate, etc.
Tripartite schemas, on the other hand, must have appeared to him as of
an *erudite* nature, tools of those clerics proudly puffed up with their
knowledge, of those people glutted with culture that horrified him.
To these tripartite schemas, furthermore, were connected the notions
of hierarchy that gravitated around the term *ordo*. In the schema, classic
since the eleventh century, of the tripartite society, the third order, that
of the *laboratores*, was subject to the two higher orders of *oratores* and
bellatores, just as in Genesis Ham was subjected by God to Shem and
Japhet.[50]

What is more, Saint Francis employed the term 'order' only in the
sense of the ecclesiastical Orders, as a purely technical term, or, after
he was forced to give up the concept of a fraternity – a significant
conflict – to describe his Order of Minors.

On the other hand, his biographers use the term 'order' in connection
with a tripartite schema. But, in one case, what is meant is the three
orders founded by Saint Francis: the Friars Minor, the Poor Clares
and the Third Order.[51] In the other, it is stated that the Franciscan
doctrine assures the salvation of all orders, all genders and all ages.[52]
Thus, in the first case, the term is employed outside any ideological
reference. In the second, if it indeed designates, contrary to the use
by Saint Francis himself, all social categories, it was associated in the

saint's mind with notions of age and gender that attenuate its ideological scope.

Thus, between the single and hierarchical celestial world and the
social multiplicity of a disorderly, terrestrial world, Francis dreamt of
instituting Franciscan society as a mediator, whose structure should
be the negation and the conversion of earthly disorder.

In the biographies

The biographies of Saint Francis include both people who constitute
groups or categories which can be listed and that sometimes even
appear in a list, and individuals designated by their social category, but
in an isolated or even unusual manner.

The lists

The groups or social categories that appear very frequently in the biographies of Saint Francis belong to three series: the *audiences* of the
saint, the *hosts* who received him and the *beneficiaries* or *witnesses* of
his miracles.

THE AUDIENCES

What predominates very naturally in the description of the audiences is
again the concern for totality, designed to show that the sermons of the
saint addressed everyone and that his success was universal. Although
the biographers give details only of the Italian apostolate, which did
in fact absorb most of Saint Francis's missionary life, they emphasise
the actual territorial formations to which this apostolate gave rise: a
geographical totality here too. But the model, if it corresponds to
reality, is always evangelical and christological: Saint Francis travels
through 'towns and villages' ('civitates et castella'), the terms employed
by the Gospels to describe the apostolate of Jesus.[53] Under these conditions, is it possible to engage in a valid exegesis of the vocabulary
to try to determine whether Francis's apostolate extended as much to
a rural as to an urban environment?[54] In any case, the evangelical
terms were very apposite to the type of habitat grouped into the cities
and semi-urban country towns in central and northern Italy. The

prototype of the social and geographical milieu where Franciscan preaching predominantly took place was Assisi. This type of small town situated near the major roads that were wide open to the rural environment is, moreover, very representative of a large part of the medieval West.[55]

The point must nevertheless be made that the biographers' enumerations, in their desire to emphasise that social differences and antagonisms vanished before the high reputation of the saint, foreground these splits and tensions inside society even more than the words of the saint himself.

The schema is that of the saint's arrival in a built-up area. To cries of: 'The saint is coming, here is the saint', the population assembles – generally in the main square – to see him, to touch him, to hear him. Sometimes the biographers merely say that 'the whole population' or 'everyone' – 'universus populus'[56] – was there. More often, they are specific. The saint mainly addresses the lay people,[57] but he attracts clerics as well. The presence of both regular and secular clerics is a detail meant to show the esteem in which Francis was held by the clergy, or better, the reputation that the saint enjoyed among it. Here one of the great barriers of medieval society, that which separated the clergy from the laity, is being removed.[58] Similarly, people of all ages and both genders hurry forward – an innocuous detail at first glance, which nevertheless reveals that in medieval society women and, to a lesser degree, the elderly were undervalued social categories.[59] From a viewpoint closer to the modern concept of social structure in historical societies, Francis brings together the two opposing groups of the poor and the rich ('divites–pauperes') and *above all* (this is visibly the greatest social division from the biographers' viewpoint) the *nobles* and the *non-nobles* ('nobiles–ignobiles').[60] In an interesting text, written in verse, Henri d'Avranches opposes 'pauper' not to 'dives' but to 'potens' and, adding to this the cultural divide, 'simplex' not to 'litteratus' but to 'peritus', showing that social superiority issues from a power that is more than wealth and from a technical knowledge (specialists in law and mechanical arts?) that exceeds clerical culture.[61]

In another text, Thomas of Celano makes a detailed list of all the faithful, of all types and qualities ('quicumque ac qualiscumque'), that comprise Francis's typical audience: these are the 'rich' and the 'poor', the 'noble' and the 'non-noble', the 'ordinary man' and the 'man of quality' ('vilis–carus'), the 'knowing man' and the 'simple man' ('prudens–simplex'), and the 'cleric' and the 'unlettered',[62] a true summary of the conscious divisions within society.

THE HOSTS

It is surely unnecessary to draw overly strict conclusions from the fact that, with a few exceptions (the 'poor priest of San Damiano', the monks of Gubbio), the hosts of Saint Francis that his biographers designate by a social term all belong to the upper groups. They are the most impressively memorable ones, whose mention shows that the Franciscan circles wanted to emphasise the impact produced by Saint Francis on the upper crust of society. These are the lords ('domini'),[63] and the great ('magnae personae').[64] If it was the 'magni principes' who invited Francis to a meal, Thomas of Celano is nevertheless eager to point out that the saint ate only half-heartedly.[65] When Henri d'Avranches has him received by those 'magnates' whom Francis unsympathetically compared to the 'gastaldi' and the demons, we must remember that we are dealing with certainly the least Franciscan of his biographers.[66] Finally, when at Tuscanella it was a knight, a 'miles', who received him, this may be another evangelical reference, an allusion to the centurion who was the host of Jesus.[67]

THE BENEFICIARIES AND WITNESSES OF MIRACLES

If those not designated by a properly 'social' term (homo, mulier, puer, puella, caecus, insanus, etc.) and animals are discounted, out of the 197 miracles reported by Thomas of Celano in his Tractatus de miraculis, sixty-two (a little less than a third) concern characters designated by their social position. But here even more than for the hosts, tradition has mainly retained the members of the higher categories. Almost half, twenty-eight, belong to the nobility or to the chivalry: 'nobilis' or 'nobiles' are mentioned eleven times, to whom must be added noble women ('nobiles mulieres' once) and a woman of great nobility ('nobilissima'); lords ('dominus' once and 'domina' twice), one great prince ('magnus princeps'), a palace count ('comes sacri palatii'), one countess ('comitissa'), two potentates ('potestas'), seven knights ('miles' five times, 'eques' once, 'duo viri loricati' once).

The society of the clerical and liberal professions is represented only six times (one 'canonicus', one 'frater praedicator', one 'scolaris', one 'notarius', one 'officialis', one 'iudex'). The number of 'bourgeois' comes to five ('civis' four times, one 'popularis homo'). The medical world appears six times ('medicus' four times, 'chirurgicus' once, and once 'mulieres edoctae', who were probably midwives). Rural society is represented six times: besides one 'rusticus', one 'arator' and one 'vir cum bobus', two 'vinitores' and one 'piscator' must be added. Sailors ('nautae') appear twice, servants twice (one 'serviens', one 'famula'), tradesmen a single time, and there again as bell-founders ('fusores campanarum'). Finally, the poor are mentioned only six times ('pauper' twice, 'mendicus' twice, one 'pauperculus', one 'vetula extrema paupertate').

The rare and the unusual

We are here grouping the social types mentioned in the biographies of Saint Francis in addition to the groups or categories studied above, and terms that pose a problem, either because they give rise to controversial questions concerning the social condition and the social ideology of Saint Francis, or because they offer unexpected insights.

THE RARE: RUSTICUS, ARTIFEX, LATRONES

Absent or poorly represented in the lists that mainly include members of urban gatherings are the peasants who more often met Francis on lonely paths: the candid and mischievous 'rusticus' who advised the saint to be worthy of the greatness of his reputation;[68] the confident 'rusticus' who followed the saint, climbing to a hermitage in the summer dog-days, and for whom Francis made refreshing water spring from a rock;[69] the gross and hostile 'rusticus' who pushed his donkey into the little hut of Francis and his first companions on the Rivo Torto to chase them out.[70]

A surprising rarity, we encounter in the biographies but a single 'artifex'[71] – and again, he may be there only because Celano met the expression 'egregius artifex' in the Bible (Exodus 38:23).

Another unique encounter was that with the bandits who threw Francis into the snow, in one of the famous episodes of his life.[72] Outlaws were very familiar in medieval society, but these ones seem to have been especially marshalled by the biographer for the reply, 'I am the herald of the great King.' 'Go then, peasant, you who think you're

God's herald.'[73] Was he a herald or a jester – (*joculator*) of God, as he was called later? Did Francis appear in this adventure as a character of the world of spiritual chivalry to which he has long been connected, or as one of those vile professionals, one of the despised *mercenarii* among whom he liked to be counted?

THE DOUBTFUL CASE OF THE ORIGINAL SOCIAL TYPE OF SAINT FRANCIS: *MILES* OR *MERCATOR*?

That Francis was the son of a cloth merchant, itinerant as were such merchants at the beginning of the thirteenth century, there is no doubt. That he had led in his youth a chivalrous lifestyle, whose practice, as Marc Bloch has ably shown, sometimes permitted him to slip into the knightly class itself, is also certain, so that when he was taken prisoner by the Perugians, he shared the gaol of the knights.[74] Thomas of Celano insisted on this contradiction in the first episodes of the biography, making Francis a prudent merchant like those of his class, yet generous like the nobles,[75] and recalling in particular the vanity of his chivalrous dreams: when he sees in a dream a house full of weapons, the biographer declares that it would have been more suitable for him to see one filled with piles of cloth.[76]

Once converted, Francis – as we have seen – avoided mentioning, either for himself or for others, these *milites* whose vanity and violence he reproved, and these *mercatores* whose love of money he condemned. It even happened that he made a point of his mediocre origin, as in the episode of the ride with Brother Leonard.[77] Francis was riding the only donkey, while Leonard was walking by his side, on foot. Leonard, dissatisfied, was thinking to himself, 'His parents and mine did not play together as equals. And here he is riding while I am on foot and leading his donkey.' The saint surmised his thoughts and, dismounting, said to him, 'My brother, it is not right that I should ride and you should walk, for in the world you were more noble and powerful than I.' 'Nobilior et potentior': Francis, despite everything, employed a comparative that reveals that even when he recognised the earthly hierarchies, he rejected the impermeability of the classes.

It remains that most of his biographers reserved the terms 'miles' and 'mercator' (or 'negotiator') to apply them to him with a spiritual meaning, after his conversion. This was because these words belonged to the traditional hagiographical vocabulary, with the reservation that 'negotiator', a term of the high Middle Ages, generally replaced 'mercator', which had not yet gained respectability. Francis thus became, on the one hand, 'negotiator evangelicus',[78] and on the other, 'miles Christi',[79] 'miles fortissimus in castris hujus saeculi',[80] and 'doctissimus miles in castris Dei'.[81] The poetic and non-Franciscan authors were those who most applied to Francis a military and chivalrous vocabulary that did not suit him. If 'dux' was employed not only by Henri d'Avranches,[82] but also by Julian of Speyer[83] and Saint Bonaventure,[84] the grand prize for the transfiguration of Francis goes to Pope Gregory IX in the sequence *Caput draconis* composed in honour of the Poverello, who there became 'princeps inclytus'.[85]

THE EQUIVOCAL CASE OF THE *MAGISTRI* AND *DOCTORES*: SAINT FRANCIS AND THE UNIVERSITY SCHOLARS

A full discussion of the attitude of Saint Francis to scholarship and scholars, and in particular the relations between the Minors and the universities, would take us too far from our topic. Besides, it would be necessary to engage in a difficult exegesis of texts, and notably the sensitive issue of the authenticity of the letter to Saint Anthony of Padua.

It seems that Francis felt at least mistrust for scholars, because he regarded knowledge as a form of possession and property, and the educated as an especially formidable section of the powerful; but his respect for the clergy in general made him extend this reverence to those of its members who were scholars. He considered theology, in particular, to mean knowledge of the Holy Scriptures, although he did not consider that learned mediation was indispensable between the Bible (especially the Gospels, of easier access) and the faithful, or at least the mediation of preachers like him and his brothers. Hence we see the statement in his *Testament*, 'We must honour and revere all the theologians and those who serve the very holy divine words.'[86] Also, Thomas of Celano was surely right in attributing to him a reverence that he nevertheless exaggerated towards the 'divinae legis doctores'.[87] Francis must have been much more reticent about the frequenting of the universities and, with even more reason, the occupation of teaching positions by the Minors. University status, whatever Thomas Aquinas and Bonaventure said later, was little conducive to the practice of poverty, both because it implied the possession of books, which were very expensive and which people did not yet recognise as having the character of professional tools,[88] and because university life made it difficult to earn a subsistence either by manual labour or by actual begging. Moreover, Thomas of Celano was explicit on this last point.[89]

It remains that the general conditions of the apostolate of the Mendicants in general and the Minors in particular developed in a way that quickly impelled the Order to frequent the universities and to revere the masters and doctors. Therefore Saint Francis's attitude to the professionals of learning was certainly profoundly misrepresented by his biographers, from Thomas of Celano to Saint Bonaventure, who had every personal and general reason for doing so. With him, the Christ of Saint Francis became chiefly a *Magister*.[90]

UNUSUAL ASSOCIATIONS OF POVERTY WITH THE UPPER STRATA

Finally, certain terms can be surprising in the mouth of Saint Francis and in the social and mental context of his era. Some, on the one hand, transformed poverty into a great Lady and some, on the other, showed the poor belonging to the upper social strata.

On the one hand, Francis made Poverty his supreme social value, a Lady, a Great Lady: this was 'Domina Paupertas',[91] 'Paupertas Altissima'.[92] This surely results from a psychological intricacy that would be difficult to analyse. First, the converted Francis remained the lover of the courtly poetry of his youth; the jongleur of God was especially the lover of Poverty, which appeared to him, according to Saint Bonaventure, sometimes as a mother, sometimes as a spouse, sometimes as a Lady or rather a mistress.[93] He identified, moreover, so much with his Lady that he became Her and was recogniszed one day as such by three poor women (possible influence of folklore) who greeted him: '*Domina Paupertas*'. Then, he wanted to enshrine the mysticism of Poverty by presenting it with the characteristics of the highest cultural and social model of his time: the Lady, whom the Virgin Mary also incarnated. Finally, in his enterprise to overturn the social ideology, in his social and spiritual revolution, he was doubtless pleased to elevate to the first rank, in a movement that was still evangelical, that which society placed and which placed itself last.

Due place should be given to the episode obligingly told by Thomas of Celano and Saint Bonaventure[94] of the meeting of Saint Francis with the poor knight ('miles pauper') to whom he gave his clothing. The meaning of the story is clear in the intention of the hagiographers. It is a matter of – and Thomas of Celano takes full advantage of this – comparing Saint Francis with Saint Martin in a manner favourable to the one who gave everything, while the other gave only half. However, from a properly Franciscan perspective, it is a matter of making a major example of this real social type, a type that transcends secular stratification and represents a category in which poverty and nobility are united in a gloriously shocking manner – a living incarnation of the ideology of the Franciscan social utopia.

Interpretative essay

The preceding pages have already initiated some explanatory and interpretative schemas, as it would have been difficult to remain limited to a simple inventory or a pure description. We would nevertheless like to outline here a more systematic approach to the semantic material that we have presented.

Situation of this vocabulary in relation to medieval ideological schemas

If, in the social vocabulary of Saint Francis and his first biographers, we look for the relationships that we proposed examining in the 'Outline for the Historical Study of the Social Vocabulary of the Medieval West', which appeared in *Ordres et classes*, we observe the following.

The closed qualitative schemas scarcely appear. In Saint Francis, the tripartite schema retains the *oratores* and *laboratores* but has lost the *bellatores*. The *omnis ordo, omnis aetas, omnis sexus* triad, encountered once in Thomas of Celano, is unusual and does not seem to imply a specific ideology.

The quantitative schemas 'of the Aristotelian type' are better represented, but without rigidity, either because they break up into several combinations, or because they depart from the usual patterns. For example, other equivalent pairs in which *prudens, sapiens, peritus, clericus* stand on one side, and *simplex, idiota, rusticus* and *inutilis* on the other, reproduce the *litterati–illiterati* pair. *Potens*, as well as *dives*, can be the opposite of *pauper*. The *Minores* are implicitly contrasted to all the others who must be *majores*, but these 'majors' are generally not named. More than in antithetical and complementary pairs, Francis and, to a lesser degree, his biographers, are interested in bringing out equivalent pairs that reveal relatively unexpected social connections, but that are not always opposed, in any case explicitly, by pairs of antithetical equivalents. Thus, alongside 'pauperes et illiterati', to which 'divites et sapientes' are symmetrically opposed (*Vita secunda*, 193, p. 241), 'idiotae et subditi' (*Testamentum*, 4), 'sapientiores et potentiores' (*Epistola ad populorum rectores*), 'servi et subditi' (*Epistola ad fideles*, 9), and 'nobilior et potentior' (Francis in Bonaventure, *Legenda major*, XI, 8, p. 608) are sufficient in themselves.

The qualitative open lists are the best represented, with the proviso that they tend to embrace the social totality. But this quantitative aim is more subjective and mystical than mathematical, since it happens that, at least in one case (I *Regula*, XXIII), the same people are accounted for several times through the interplay of the accumulated groups defined by different criteria.

In fact, the type of society that appears through the Franciscan schemas is a shattered society showing the remains of various structures, but in fragments. In the present study, we are seeking to bring out elements of real combinations of structures that differ from the ordinary combinations of language and we are suggesting the possibility of a greater fragmentation of society by the play of open qualitative lists. But our tendency is to collect all the fragments together.

Before asking, 'What can possibly be restructured from them?' we must situate this Franciscan vocabulary in relation to other medieval vocabularies.

How this vocabulary relates to the main specific social vocabularies of the Middle Ages

To 'feudal' vocabulary

The terms *dominus, servus, miles*, etc. are used but *homo, vasallus, vavassor, liber*, etc., are not. The use of *dominus, servus* and *miles* seems due to their long semantic history and, in particular, their presence in biblical vocabulary. This absence of 'feudal' vocabulary is certainly largely due to the more relaxed character of properly feudal institutions in Italy. The important consequence is the weak impact of this vocabulary on Franciscan terminology.

To 'political' vocabulary

We have already noted how little monarchic terminology is used: *imperator, rex, regina, principes, magnati*, etc. The 'communal' vocabulary (*potestas, civis, homo popularis*, etc.) is just as little used. With his political pessimism (mentioned above), Saint Francis avoided language of a political type.

To 'religious' vocabulary

Both qualitatively and quantitatively, religious vocabulary seems the most significant. The basic *clerici–laici* classification, the liturgical terminology, and the considerations of gender and age were as many references, as many borrowings from the language of the Church – not surprisingly from the founder of an essentially religious and Catholic movement. However, his mistrust of *litterati*, which was one reason why Saint Francis rejected learned ideological schemas, his desire that his Order and his faithful should be apart not of course from the Church but from clericalism, and the constant use of non-religious alongside the religious terminology whose insufficiency is thus demonstrated: all this shows that the social vocabulary of Franciscanism also escaped if not the religious, at least the ecclesiastical, mould.

Other influences

There may be some interest in observing, without drawing any conclusions, that some key words of the social vocabulary of Franciscanism are, if not borrowed from, at least the same as those of a certain legal language that had passed into current use, on the one hand, and those of the terminology of the trades and professional services that were coming into being, on the other.

The first of these categories includes legal terms mostly borrowed from the Bible and that can be found in the twelfth to thirteenth centuries both in the writings of jurists and in current vocabulary. An example is *subditi*, which medieval political and legal thinking and vocabulary had doubtless borrowed from Saint Paul (Titus 3:1, 'Admonish them to be *obedient* to the princes and the powerful' ('Admone illos principibus et potestatibus *subditos* esse').[95] This word was connected with a morality and a spirituality of obedience that blossom in Saint Francis's work after a long and constant medieval tradition.[96]

One text in particular points to the connection which is basic to an understanding of Franciscan vocabulary, that between *subditi* and *minores*. Guido Faba wrote in a formulary of around 1230: 'If the great, clergy or laity, ecclesiastical prelates or secular lords, make known in writing to the *subjects or to the minors*' ('Si majores, clerici vel laici, prelati ecclesiastici vel domini saeculares, *subditis vel minoribus* scripserint', and one of the chapters had the title 'Principia de subditis et minoribus'.[97]

At around the same time, two other formularies – the *Summa dictaminum* of Ludolf and the *Formulary* of Baumgartenberg – define *personae minores* as follows: 'merchants, simple citizens, those who practise the mechanical arts [manual trades] and all those who like them are lacking in dignities' ('mercatores, cives simplices, et artis mechanicae professores et omnes consimiles carentes dignitatibus').[98] This is the very essence of the vocabulary of Franciscanism, its atmosphere, and its society.

From another perspective, when Francis wrote a letter '*ad populorum rectores*' and called the superiors of his Order's convents 'custodes', the corporations, which were then in the process of establishing their statutes, gave their leaders the title 'rectores' or 'custodes', as for example in Toulouse, in 1227.[99] The word 'minister' that Francis so much liked to apply to himself and to his brothers then designated apprentices in the trades, also called 'discipuli' or 'laboratores' (or 'laborantes'). Organised trades were then called 'ministeria' rather than *artes*, a word which did later gain precedence in Italy and whose semantic field is completely different.[100]

Thus, extending the research beyond the Franciscan authors brings out latent connections with the juridical and religious vocabulary of contemporary life, and with the professional and corporative vocabulary of the world of trades.

We can now attempt to define the goals of Franciscanism through its social vocabulary, because as much as it is a description of the society on which it wants to act, the vocabulary of an ideology is an instrument of the transformation of this society.

How this vocabulary relates to the Franciscan vision and aims[101]

Initial antagonisms

Although Saint Francis strove to avoid using set pairs of opposites, it is clear that the starting point of his social vision was a two-part one, founded on inequality. That the *pauper*, the *egenus* or the *idiota* was the opposite of the *dives*, the *potens* or the *sapiens* was not, in fact, the main point. Most important was the gap separating the two groups, inside each of which the labels and those who wore them were basically interchangeable, since they were often the same: poverty, indigence and ignorance go hand in hand, as do wealth, power and knowledge on the other side of the fence.

In his social vocabulary, Francis was simply extending the opposition between two parties whose history, which he had experienced at Assisi in his youth and then found again in all his travels, appeared to him as the very fabric of social structure and activity.

Whether or not his knightly culture added anything to the image, he conceived the society that he wanted to convert and to transform in the form of a duel, a class struggle between two sides. According to Thomas of Celano (*Vita secunda*, 37, p. 153), what he had seen in Perugia provided him with a starting point: 'Saeviunt in milites populares, et verso gladio nobiles in plebeios.' The political and social terms *milites–populares*, *nobiles–plebei*, constitute the basic pairs of opposites. This symmetrical antagonism does not allow for an aggressor and an aggressed, but it must be noted that force – here the sword – introduced an equality among the upper classes, favouring them and creating an imbalance.

The struggle for equality

Francis aimed to replace these antagonisms with a society founded on family relationships, in which the only inequalities would be based on age and gender – natural inequalities and therefore divine. Hence his mistrust or hostility towards all those who raise themselves above others through social artifices. The enemies of Saint Francis were those whose designations included prefixes marking superiority: *magis-* (*magnus*, *magister*, *magnatus*), *prae-* (*praelatus*, *prior*), *super-* (*superior*).[102] Those to be exalted in compensation were the people society undervalued: *minores* and *subditi*.

The supreme social evil was power. The best definition of an abusive man was *potens*. Whatever the basis of this power, it had to be, if not destroyed, then at least neutralised.

The first such basis was birth, and this seems to have been the least objectionable in Saint Francis's view, perhaps because, being innate, it had something natural about it and, in a certain way, came from God.

The two other bases – more abominable because they were acquired through effort and will – were wealth and knowledge. Social climbing was the great social sin, and its two stepping stones, money and culture, had to be avoided at all costs, except to the limited extent that the one is necessary for subsistence and the other for salvation, that is, chiefly for the understanding of Holy Scripture.

The social ideal to which Francis aspired was levelling, maximum equality at the humblest level. He fully recognised that there was no hope of achieving this in society as a whole, but he wanted to establish it in his 'fraternity'. Here, Francis was in a long-standing tradition of the monasticism that had always conceived, albeit in different ways, monastic society – either the monastery or the Order – as a *social model*.[103] But in order to achieve his goal fully, Francis would have wished his model to transcend the division and opposition between clergy and laity. In receiving members of both among his brothers, he hoped to create a society on a completely original model that was neither wholly secular nor, more important still, wholly ecclesiastic. He was not allowed to do this.

Saint Francis always emphasised this *uniformitas*, particularly, perhaps, by way of compensation when he had to accept that the structure of an Order had been imposed on him. On this point, his biographers generally have been faithful to his thinking.

Thomas of Celano gives due weight to this *societas caritatis* that he wanted to create among his brothers by means of a *uniformitas* that would make the disparities between *maiores* and *minores*, *litterati* and *illiterati* disappear.[104] The biographer of the *Legenda monacensis* recalls how the saint wanted to introduce terminology that would eliminate and offset the inequality of functions and positions inside the Order by replacing the terms *abbot*, *provost* and *prior* with those of *minister* and *custodian*.[105]

Saint Bonaventure, finally, emphasised that Francis rejected Gregory IX's idea that the brothers should be promoted to ecclesiastical ranks (*dignitates*, *praelationes*), on the grounds that they should retain the *status* (should this word *status*, little used by Saint Francis be regarded as a social term?) of their *vocation* (*vocatio*, a term that has the desired equivalence of the word and the ideal).[106]

How was this uniformity to be achieved, inside the Order and outside it? How was this 'classless society' to be realised?

If Francis dreamed of launching his brothers into political struggle, he only wanted to have them play the role of *peacemakers*.[107] Although he sometimes pronounced subversive slogans, supported moreover by scriptural authority (such as '*Ego fur esse nolo*'[108] that evokes the famous 'Property is theft'), he in fact never dreamed of using force or even political power which, as we have seen, he regarded as an eminently suspect form of power.

The reason was that this man, contemptuous of inequalities and hierarchies, was also, and in his Order in the first place, a passionate apostle of *obedience*. This ideal of obedience underlay the choice of submission, and was the justification and the ideal of the voluntary *subditus*.

From the perspective of action on the society in which Saint Francis lived, what could this obedience be called today, if not *non-violence*? It was through the subversive, shocking and revolutionary nature of this voluntary submission that Francis and his own hoped to transform society. However, this obedience was not blind, because obedience can be bad if it responds automatically without examining the value of what it is accepting. Even, in fact especially, inside his Order, Francis warned his brothers against this false obedience that puts itself in the service of crime or of sin[109] and preached, on the contrary, 'the true and holy obedience', 'vera et sancta obedientia'. Moreover, in the revised Rule that was imposed on him, he was obliged to weaken this recommendation considerably. But he was only making discipline subject to the casuistry that was developing in his time around notions and practices until then condemned or praised *in themselves*. Now people were trying to define a licit and an illicit domain, or a just and an unjust sector, in, for example, war, profit, games, idleness, work and so on.

Foundations of a new social order

However much effort it would take to achieve it, whatever its underlying positive value of eliminating injustice, this ideal of levelling down remains essentially a negative one. Furthermore, as Saint Francis tended to limit its practice to his brothers, what new order was he proposing to society?

The question is difficult to untangle and it is probable that, like many reformers and revolutionaries, Francis saw much more clearly the evil to get rid of than the good to set up in its place. We can nevertheless consider that he delivered the essence of his thinking in a declaration reported by Thomas of Celano (*Vita secunda*, 146, p. 214),

> He said: we have been sent to help the clerics, to promote the salvation of their soul, so as to provide that which they are lacking. May each receive his salary *not according to his authority, but according to his labour.*
>
> (Dicebat autem: In adjutorium clericorum missi sumus ad salutem animarum promovendam, ut quod minus invenitur in illis, suppleatur in nobis. Recipiet unusquisque mercedem *non secundum auctoritatem, sed secundum laborem.*)

Francis was taking up Saint Paul again. But he distorted or rather expanded the text of 1 Cor. 3:8 ('unusquisque autem propriam mercedem accipiet secundum suum laborem') in such a way as to replace an order founded on *rank* with an order founded, let us say, on labour, on *merit*. But how should *labor* be translated?

An attempt to outline the attitudes of Saint Francis and his contemporaries to *work* goes beyond the scope of this book. It must suffice to say that, faced with developments that tended to eliminate the strictly moral harmonics of *labor* (pains), emphasising instead its socio-professional and socio-economic overtones, Saint Francis does not seem to have chosen a clear definition, a failure that can easily be explained by the undermining of language, itself a reflection of the confused state of economic and social institutions.[110]

Language is an instrument in the hands of people and of societies, but it is also a structure imposed on them. As well as being inflexible in itself, it makes infrastructures inflexible.

How this vocabulary relates to the problematics of a historian

Just as the analysis and description of the elements of the Franciscan social vocabulary are matters of interpretation, the effort to elucidate the meaning of this vocabulary for Saint Francis and his contemporaries depends to some degree on the situation of the historian who approaches it with his own set of tools and problematics. In conclusion therefore it is only fair, in fact necessary, to attempt, at least briefly, to be explicit on this point.

The historical context

The specific time and the specific place are crucial: the Italian soil of Franciscanism gave it a terrain where the feudal system in the classic sense had never really existed and where, sooner and more strongly than elsewhere, an urban social model became predominant, characterised by confrontation between two *parties*.

But even more significantly, at the turn from the twelfth to thirteenth century, in Western Christendom as a whole, though some places were in advance and others were backward to different degrees and in different modalities, a general social reclassification was taking place. This upheaval was felt in terms of power, and a new division was established between those who participated in the new forms of power and those who were excluded from it. Let us note, without going into details, that the spread of the money economy, both a result and a cause of this upheaval, was sufficient neither to explain it nor to define it. Money did not play the central role in this social revolution, any more than it was the main protagonist of the Franciscan social and ideological theatre.[111] Money was but one of the elements of the new power, just as nobility, inversely, remained one of its essential components.

In this redistribution of social categories, the stratum that lost out was that of the *subditi*, the subject or the obedient, who were also called *pauperes*, because poverty is not only the opposite of wealth. This has always been true, but here a new class of poor had emerged, and a new and an unprecedented pauperisation of society.[112] Just as in the tripartite schema, which the clergy used to describe the society that was now passing, the *laboratores* could represent either the whole undervalued category or only its upper layer – a rural economic elite kept away from power – in the new system the *personae minores* could designate either, as in Saint Francis's tendency, the whole lower layer, *minores* thus becoming synonymous with *subditi* and *pauperes*, or, as in the formularies cited in note 4 on p. 135, an elite, this one urban, but also lacking the dignities, functions, attributes and advantages of power.

Choice of the system of references

What sociological and ideological model can be used to define such a society?

Without entering into the details of complex systems which in any case seldom came into being in their pure form in the history of real societies, we can briefly state that this society was neither one of *castes*, nor one of *orders*, nor one of *classes*. Keeping to very general criteria, this detailed analysis of the Franciscan vocabulary of social categories and the realities that it covered has shown that they had neither the character of sacred or religious stratification of castes and orders, nor the relative homogeneity of classes.

It seems that the sociological mode most apt to analyse such a society – and one of the historical merits of Franciscanism is to have emphasised this through the primordial significance granted to the depreciated strata – is that of *pauperism*, in the sense in which Oscar Lewis, for instance, speaks of the culture of pauperism.

But pauperism is not an exact term, and in conclusion we must briefly examine what type of 'pauperist society' is profiled behind the social vocabulary of Franciscanism.

Definition of the problem

The pauperist society of the Western low Middle Ages that burst to the fore of the historical scene through Franciscanism and its vocabulary was not segregationist, despite the chasm that separated the powerful from the poor. Unlike the isolated American cultures of pauperism studied by Oscar Lewis, medieval pauperist society was caught up in the current of development and growth.

The basic problem that Saint Francis and his companions wanted to solve was how to integrate this pauperist society into history. Of course, their solution, which cannot possibly be analysed here beyond the social and linguistic study outlined above, was a religious solution, a spiritual one: integration, history and salvation. Although Franciscanism – and the broader religious movement to which it must be attached – made a deep impression on the world of the low Middle

Ages and continues today to be present and active in Western culture, its social solution was a failure.

The problem for the historian is therefore to look beyond the ambition and the failure of Franciscanism, and try to find a model of historical growth that explains the outcome of this pauperist society. Two integrationist processes can be identified that made it possible for this society to become wholly involved in development.

One was economic. The advance of the money economy and of accumulation which affected – though very unequally, of course – all categories of society, first created a new pauperism (that of the industrial revolution, instead of making a positive imprint on society, as in the low Middle Ages, was on the contrary merely its negative), and then made it possible for the pauperist society to accede to the present consumer economy.

The other was politico-cultural. The formation of national unities and national consciousnesses prevented the undervalued social categories from remaining in the ghetto where they were in danger of being enclosed by a Christian unity that had become formalised, having lost its material and psychic dynamism.[113]

Where the social vocabulary of the original Franciscanism has its best historical insights is in the place it grants open qualitative schemas that interpreted and facilitated the integration of pauperist society, which it also well defined, into the march of history.

In this sense, the following explanatory historical statement, succinct but still scientifically effective, can be made: the social vocabulary of the original Franciscanism was representative of the transitional phase from feudalism to capitalism, according to the original modalities characteristic of this phase in medieval Western society.[114]

✤ 4 ✤

FRANCISCANISM AND CULTURAL MODELS OF THE THIRTEENTH CENTURY

The purpose of this chapter is to establish a list of models or key concepts characteristic of the prevailing mentality and sensibility of the
thirteenth century and to attempt to define the attitude of the Franciscans towards these models in their mission to secular society. Achieving
this purpose presents two sets of difficulties.

The first lies in the definition of cultural models. These are usually
developed by the ruling social strata: the clerics and nobles. It is very
difficult to have access to the properly 'popular' models, not those
that are simply received by the dominated rural and urban social
strata – popularised models – but those that are proper to the traditional
culture of these strata, let us say the 'folk' culture. I have taken a special
interest in the models that appeared to me to pervade the whole of
society, the 'common' models.

In the Middle Ages, there was no specific domain of culture in the
modern sense of the term. The expression 'cultural models' is used
here in a broad sense and the key concepts of the value systems are considered from the viewpoint of historical anthropology. I have particularly focused on new values or values that became prevalent in the
thirteenth century. I have retained the following models:

- models related to the perception of space and time: cities, churches,
  houses, novelty and memory;
- models related to the evolution of the economy: money and work;

This chapter was first published as a paper in *Atti dell'VIII Convegno della Società internazionale di studi francescani: Francescanesimo e vita religiosa dei laici nel' 200 (Assisi,
16–18 ottobre 1980)*, Assisi, 1981, pp. 85–128.

- models related to the structure of global or civil society: the 'estates' (*status*), laity, women, children and charity (works of compassion, not just the giving of alms);
- models related to the structure of religious society: prelacy and fraternity;
- models related to culture in a narrow sense: intellectual work and learning, the spoken word, vernacular language and arithmetic;
- models of behaviour and sensibility: courtesy, beauty, joy and death;
- ethical and religious models strictly speaking: penance, poverty, humility, purity (the body), prayer and saintliness;
- traditional models of the sacred: dreams and visions, miracles, witchcraft and exorcism.

I give less emphasis to those that are probably the most important but also the most familiar: penance, poverty and humility.

The second set of difficulties centres on an appreciation of Franciscan evangelisation. Its practice is different in different tendencies of the Order (in particular the movement of the Spirituals); it has been evolving ever since the lifetime of Saint Francis; it has been so strongly marked by its founder's personality that this study constantly refers back to Francis himself, and yet it has moved perceptibly from what one might suppose to have been his ideals and his behaviour. Franciscan evangelisation has not always been very clearly distinguished, either by its contemporaries or by historians of the apostolate, from all the other Mendicant Orders and, in particular, from the Dominicans. It is therefore not always easy to grasp what is innovative about the Franciscans, although this is striking in certain areas. Finally, it is necessary to take into account the distance between purported ideals and real behaviour, not in order to put the Order on trial, which is not part of the role of the historian, but because the difference between the models preached and the models really practised can pose difficult problems of interpretation on the historical role of Franciscanism concerning the laity. But in my opinion, despite the inconsistencies, contradictions and trends that I occasionally indicate, there was coherence in Franciscan values in theory and in practice in the thirteenth century; in short, there was a Franciscan model of evangelisation of the laity inside a Mendicant model.

In my inventory of the great themes of cultural life – in the broad sense – of the thirteenth century, I will evoke the attitude of the

Franciscans as an apostolate of the laity, sometimes disseminating these models or opposing them, marking them with their originality or introducing distinct new features or modifications into them.

Models related to space and time

The city

The spatial environment of Francis and the first Franciscans primarily involved alternation between city and solitude, convents and hermitages; in fact this followed the tradition of Saint Martin, oscillating between *cura animarum* as a bishop in Tours and collecting his resources as a monk in Marmoutier. Thomas of Celano laid heavy emphasis on this liking of Francis's for solitary retreats (for example, *Vita secunda*, 9: 'solitaria loca de publicis petens', 'going away from public places to find solitude').

However, the choice that Francis and his brothers made was urban apostleship. Their choice of cities and process of establishing themselves there have been well studied, principally for Italy, and more specifically for Florence[1] and Perugia.[2] In his celebrated Chronicle, Salimbene shows his interest as a Franciscan in the cities and notably in his home town of Parma. He emphasises the particular attention shown by the Franciscans to smaller towns, in contrast to the Dominicans who were more concerned with founding great convents in the more important cities.[3]

This prioritisation of cities has moreover stimulated discussions that are echoed by a Franciscan text attributed to Saint Bonaventure: the *Determinationes quaestionum super Regulam fratrum Minorum*, of which the fifth question is: 'Why do the brothers most often reside in fortified towns and urban centres?' ('Cur fratres frequentius maneant in civitatibus et oppidis?').[4] Matthew Paris even makes residing in cities a characteristic of the Minors.[5]

The spatial environment of Francis and the brothers was also a network of cities and towns and the roads between them. The Franciscans were most often *in via*, 'on the road'. The roads would lead some of them all the way to Asia and China. Of Francis and his companions, the sources say further that they went 'per civitates et loca' and penetrated into the cities and the urban centres, 'intrant civitates et villas'. Their apostleship motivated them to use or to create new community spaces in the cities, in particular for giving sermons. The new urban site for speaking was often the *square*, a civic space that was out of doors, replacing the long-gone agora and the forum of antiquity.[6] Sometimes, as in Perugia, the *bellatores*, the 'warriors', tried to appropriate this space to the detriment of the *oratores*, the 'orators'. Sometimes, as in Limoges for a speech by Anthony of Padua, the crowd was so great that it had to use the ancient Roman ruins, in this instance, the circus.[7]

Finally, the Minors (like the Preachers) became established by organising the space around and inside the cities. In the former case, the territories were delimited as centred on towns: the *custodiae* (cf. the Dominican *praedicationes*). In the latter, Clement IV's bull *Quia plerumque* of 20 November 1265 specified the minimum distance that should separate two convents of Mendicants within the same town, thus organising urban space in terms of the Mendicant convents.[8]

The church

Despite the increasing importance of the churches of the Mendicant Orders from the architectural, urban and socio-religious points of view, it must be recognised that they, and in particular the Franciscan apostolate, took little interest in the actual church building.

Pierre Michaud-Quantin has pointed out that just as the thirteenth-century universities did not attempt to possess their own buildings, so 'the Minors still seemed to consider the Portiuncula [the original humble oratory of Francis] their ideal location', and the Mendicants 'did away with the institutional and permanent ties between the cleric and the house where he resided'.[9]

A primary function of the Franciscans (as well as of the Dominicans) was *preaching*. It tended to occur outside the church, to take place *out of doors*, in the town squares, in homes, by the roadsides, wherever there were people. It created its own space for itself, or changed the *public* space into the space of the word of salvation. In this respect, the 'title' of the bull of Nicholas III of 14 August 1279, *Exiit qui seminat* ('He who sows must go out'), suggests a symbolic interpretation.

The home

The Franciscans, in their apostleship, especially in the beginning, did not wait for the laity to come to them, but they went out to the laity in their primary place of residence: the *home*.[10] Thus a phenomenon of great importance from the social and cultural viewpoint was recognised and reinforced: the constitution of the nuclear family in a specific place of residence, the recovery of the home as a centre of individual and family devotion (holy pictures, corners set aside for prayer) and, thus, of the sanctification of daily life through conversations 'at home' with religious persons. A well-known passage from *The Legend of the Three Companions* describes the birth of the Franciscan Third Order as follows, 'Likewise, husbands and wives, unable to break the bonds of marriage, devoted themselves, in their own homes, on the pious council of the Brothers, to a stricter practice of penance.'[11]

The Legend of the Three Companions, which emphasises their men of the forests/men of the cities dualism, a dualism that the first Franciscans embodied and synthesised, describes how they frequented modest homes:

> Everyone who saw them marvelled greatly, because their clothing and way of life made them very different from all the other mortals and made them, so to speak, men of the forests.
>
> Whenever they entered into a city or a castle, into a village or a modest house, they preached peace, comforted everyone, saying to fear and to love the Creator of heaven and earth and to observe his commandments.[12]

This frequenting of the homes of laymen, including nobles, knights and the rich, whom Francis himself did not disdain, because evangelism to the rich laity was equally important, if not more important, in his eyes, is related to the beginnings of the Order and the absence of specific places of hospitality.[13]

For the brothers themselves, however, the idea of possessing their own houses was certainly one of the points of tension inside the Order. Thomas of Celano tells how Francis, who had intended to travel through Bologna, learned that some brothers had recently built a house there. 'As soon as he heard the words "brothers' house", he turned on his heel, avoided Bologna and took another route; then he enjoined the brothers to leave the house immediately.'[14]

This pinpoints a change – in the direction of separation and distancing – in an important area, that of the relationships of the brothers and the laity. Apostleship in private houses and hospitality in the homes of the laity belonged especially to the first period when the brothers were still *semi-laymen*, 'visiting various houses in disseminating the word of God, following the example of the Apostles' ('cum . . . serendo semina verbi Dei apostolorum exemplo diversas circumeant mansiones'), as the bull of Honorius III of 1219 says.

Novelty

The *novel* character of Saint Francis and his Order struck his contemporaries in an epoch that had become aware that the new had a positive side and in which the traditional condemnation of novelty was being toned down.[15] A hymn in honour of Saint Francis attributed to Thomas of Celano runs

> A new order, a new model of life
> Emerges, unknown to the world.
> (Novus ordo, nova vita
> Mundo surgit inaudita.)[16]

Burchard of Ursperg, a Premonstratensian who died in 1230, says of the Minors and the Preachers in his *Chronicon*, 'While the world was getting older, two religious institutions were born in the Church to renew its youthfulness, following the example of the eagles' ('mundo jam senescente exortae sunt duae religiones in Ecclesia cujus ut aquilae renoratur juventus').[17]

In *Legenda Perusina* (*The Legend of Perugia*), Francis says to his brothers, 'And the Lord told me that I would be a new madman in the world' ('Et dixit Dominus michi quod volebat quod ego essem novellus pazzus in mundo').[18]

In his *Expositio super Regulam*, Bonaventure had to defend the Minors against the accusation of being an 'ordo fictitius, de novo institutus' ('an imagined order, instituted as a novelty') and contrasted the idea of renovation with that of innovation, 'This rule, this model of life, is not new, but is renewed' ('non est ergo haec regula aut vita nova, sed procul dubio renovata').

This 'novelty' must be located within the great reversal of values regarding time that Latin Christendom experienced between the middle of the twelfth and the middle of the thirteenth centuries.

Father Chenu has admirably shown in *La Théologie au XIIe siècle* how, in contrast with the ideology of the ageing of the world, professed in the high Middle Ages ('mundus senescit', in the phrase repeated by Burchard of Ursperg), the machine of history was set back in motion in the twelfth century. Francis de Beer has analysed with great subtlety how Thomas of Celano presents Francis as the man who saw conversion as *starting off*, emphasised by the phrase 'nunc coepi'. It is a spirituality of initiative. This movement of conversion wipes out the past, because the present and the past are antagonistic, while the present and the future are immutably one. This is particularly true from an eschatological point of view, but also in the sense of progress as a law of spiritual life: 'perfectiora incipere' (*Vita prima*, 103, 3).[19]

Even if the relationships between Franciscanism and millenarianism, or more precisely between Franciscanism and Joachimism, were close but ambiguous (notably the attempt by the Joachimites and certain tendencies among the Minors to appropriate, to interpret Franciscanism possessively), Franciscan millenarianism should not be given too much emphasis.[20] Thomas of Celano gives a very historical time-based interpretation of the Franciscan phenomenon in the Church. At Benevento when the bishop of Assisi had a vision of the dead Saint Francis, 'he called the notary and had him record the day and the hour'.[21] Such were the new habits of attention to chronological, dated time.

Memory

In societies and epochs in which *the spoken word* plays a major role – and this was true of the medieval West despite the advance of the written word – memory has an especially important function. In this regard, the art of memory underwent a renaissance in the twelfth century which reached its apogee in the thirteenth century.

The theories and techniques of memorisation proliferated and reinforced one another. The Mendicant brothers took part in this intellectual development.[22]

Christian life was more specifically defined in terms of memory. Active remembrance of Christ became an essential mainspring of spiritual life.

Confession and preaching foregrounded the *examination of conscience* that is primarily an act of remembering.

For Francis, the essential virtue was the recollection of the loving soul, the *recordatio*. Here again, Francis de Beer has shown the significance of 'recollected memory' in the conversion of Francis: 'Francis is *memor Dei*' (*Vita secunda*, 14, 15); 'he does not forget his promise' ('non obliviscetur' (*ibid.*, 11, 10)); 'he remembers Christ's wounds' ('recordans plagarum Christi' (*ibid.*, 11, 8)); 'Christ is the One who is remembered'.[23]

The conclusion of the *Regula non bullata* is an insistent appeal for the brothers to remember:

> I pray that all the brothers learn the tenor and the sense of that which has been written in this life for the salvation of our soul and recall it often to their memory. And I pray to God that He who is all-powerful, three and one, may bless all the educators, the students, the possessors, the *commemorators* and the workers.
>
> ('Rogo omnes fratres, ut addiscant tenorem et sensum eorum quae in ista vita ad salvationem animae nostrae scripta sunt et ista frequenter ad memoriam reducant. Et exoro Deum, ut ipse, qui est omnipotens, trinus et unus, benedicat omnes docentes, discentes, habentes, *recordantes* et operantes.')

Like Christ on the evening of Holy Thursday, Francis, in his testament of Siena, asked his brothers to remember him.[24]

Finally, following the tradition of early monasticism, as Athanasius said of Anthony, the act of remembering took the place of books for him, 'memoriam pro libris habebat' (*Vita secunda*, 102, 9). This is another example of the tension between anti-intellectual tendencies and participation in bookish, academic knowledge.

The memory of the Passion remained with Francis for ever after Christ spoke to him (*Vita secunda*, 11, 7), 'as if he had always had it before his eyes' ('quasi semper coram oculis'). The same inspiration animated Saint Bonaventure in his concept of *assidua devotio*.[25]

Models related to the evolution of the economy

The beginning of the thirteenth century represented a major turning point in the Western economy. Two important phenomena belong as much within the framework of ideologies and mental attitudes as within that of economic realities: the massive dissemination of the money economy and of currency, and the transformation of work, with the division of labour in the cities, the expansion of salaried work, the enhanced value placed on work, and discussions on manual labour within monastic and university society.

Money

Francis and his brothers first perceived money in its physical form, in the shape of coins that everyone, especially in the towns, had increasing opportunity to touch, to feel and to possess.

The action of rejecting money was thus first a gesture of physical repulsion, the rejection of the monetary material: coins should be considered and treated as stones and valued no more than dust. The lengthy chapter eight of the *Regula non bullata* forbids the brothers to receive money, mentioning the Devil and calling money dust ('we do not concern ourselves with this money any more than with the dust that we tread under our feet, because it is vanity of vanities' ('de his non curemus tanquam de pulvere, quem pedibus calcamus, quia, vanitas vanitatum'). It anathematises any brother who would amass or possess money and thus be a false brother, an apostate, a thief, a robber, a hoarder of treasure (he who manipulates purse-strings, treasure, 'loculos habens'), like Judas (John 14:6). The curia reduced this chapter, making the prohibition milder and shorter in the *Regula bullata*, IV, 'I firmly order all the brothers not to receive coins or money in any way, either personally or through a third party' ('Praecipio firmiter fratribus universis ut nullo modo denarios vel pecuniam recipiant per se vel per interpositam personam'). As Noonan has noted, while there was a distinction in the thirteenth century for the use of money between *usus facti* and *usus juris* ('use in fact' and 'use by law'), the Franciscans would consider that a donor could always take his money back before it was used.[26] Mistrust, at least on the theoretical plane, would persist.

Nevertheless, the Order did adapt. Not only inside the Order would the regulated use of money, excluding individual property, no longer be accursed, but also, above all, justification of its rightful acquisition and proper use would be an essential aspect of the apostolate of the Franciscans in secular society. Even more than the Dominicans, the Franciscans would accept money and people of money as part of the Christian system, and would reconcile the merchant-banker with

the Church and Christianity. In the spiritual and canonical literature of
the thirteenth century, in which the Franciscans play such an important
role as authors and disseminators – for example, in the treatises *De
casibus conscientiae* and *De virtutibus et vitiis*, the manuals for confession,
Summae confessorum, and the tracts on usury and the restitution of illicit
gains, *De usuris*, *De restititionibus* – the Franciscans, as the most prominent of all the Mendicant Orders, see a role for God and a role for the
Devil, and a role for the good and a role for the bad Christian in the
possession and use of money.[27]

Noonan has remarked that it was a Minor, Astesanus, the minister of
the Franciscan province of Lombardy who died in 1330, who provided
in his *Summa* (1317) 'the most liberal theological treatment yet given of
several debated topics [in the monetary and economic area]'.[28]

Work

Saint Francis and the brothers mainly considered work in the context of
their means of subsistence: manual labour or begging.

Francis had discussed the problem in chapter seven of the *Regula non
bullata*. He agreed that brothers who had a trade upon entering the
Order should continue to exercise it and, here again, we see the near
absence of any boundary between the laity and the brothers at that
time. Francis had even accepted the ownership of work tools ('ferra-
menta et instrumenta suis artibus opportuna', 'objects of iron and the
instruments pertinent to these works') for brother tradesmen. He
excluded from this all dishonest professions, of which the number was,
in any case diminishing at the time,[29] and quoted the biblical authorities that constituted the main arguments for giving enhanced value to
work: Psalm 127:2 – 'You will eat the fruit of your labours and be
happy' ('Labores fructuum tuorum manducabis, beatus es et bene tibi
erit') – and Saint Paul – 'He who does not want to work will not eat'
('Qui non vult operari non manducet') (2 Thess. 3:10), 'May each
remain in the office and the service to which he has been called'
('Unusquisque qui [in ea arte et officio] in quo vocatus est, permaneat')
(1 Cor. 7:24). However, one aspect worried him: salaried work. It was
forbidden to the brothers to receive a salary in money. The one prohibition that remained in the *Regula bullata*, V, concerned 'the remu-
neration of work for oneself and one's brothers' ('de mercede, laboris

pro se et suis fratribus'). In the *Testament*, manual labour is once again prescribed:

> And I myself worked with my hands, and I want to work this way; and I firmly want all the other brothers to work at an honest labour. May those who do not know how learn, not for the desire of receiving any pay for their work, but as an example and to combat laziness.
>
> (Et ego manibus meis laborabam, et volo laborare; et omnes alii fratres firmiter volo, quod laborent de laboritio, quod pertinet ad honestatem. Qui nesciunt, discant, non propter cupiditatem recipiendi pretium laboris, sed propter exemplum et ad repellendam otiositatem.)
>
> *(Testament, 20–1)*

Richard de Bonington, in his *Tractatus de Paupertate fratrum minorum* (verses 1311–13), places the Franciscans on the side of the active, working life in the great divide between it and contemplative life ('they lead an active life as much as possible, that is, a life of labour' ('vacant ut plurimum actioni, que es vita laboriosa').

Brother Giles, to avoid eating his bread without working ('otiose'), went to fetch water at a spring, carried it in a jug on his shoulder, and went to the city to give it in exchange for bread. And to a cardinal who was surprised to see him earning his bread as a poor man, he cited Psalm 127.[30]

Thomas of Eccleston mentioned that the second layman who entered the Order in England, Laurence of Beauvais, 'worked first as a craftsman, according to the principle of the rule'.[31]

Saint Bonaventure attempted to update the tripartite schema of *oratores*, *bellatores*, *laboratores*, the outcome of the society of monks, warriors and peasants of the high Middle Ages, by relating it to contemporary urban society and intellectual patterns marked by the influences of ancient philosophy. He thus spoke of 'opus artificiale', 'opus civile', and 'opus spirituale', grouping farmers and tradesmen in the first category, in a classification of society according to activity.[32]

I merely recall that when Saint Bonaventure and Saint Thomas defended the Mendicant university masters against the secular masters, notably Guillaume de Saint-Amour, Bonaventure had to refute the accusation of idleness and thus extend the idea of work into the intellectual and religious area.[33]

Not only did the Franciscans themselves move away from the practice of manual labour and from the ideology of work, but also they paid less attention to integrating the work of the laity into the new systems of religious and spiritual values than they did to the subject of the handling of money. This is a failure of their apostolate with respect to secular society.

Models related to the structure of global or civil society

The estates (status)

The thirteenth century was a time of global inclusiveness. Exclusions were made (of Jews, heretics, lepers, etc.), but it was believed that all Christians should be included in a single structure. Francis and the Franciscans finally joined in the exclusion of certain people (heretics), although the struggle against heresy had as a theoretical goal the abjuration and the reintegration of heretics. They affirmed the place of certain rejected people in the global Christian society (lepers). They especially wanted to address themselves to the whole of society, hence the letters of Saint Francis to *all* the faithful ('First Letter to the Faithful' and 'Second Letter to the Faithful'), to *all* the clergy ('First Letter to the Clergy' and 'Second Letter to the Clergy') and to *all* the rulers ('A Letter to Rulers of the Peoples).[34]

An essential text that will not be analysed here,[35] which appeared in the *Regula non bullata* (XXIII, 7), shows Saint Francis seeking to embrace this totality of human society and reveals to us the vision he had of its structure. This passage is quoted here in full:

> Et Domino Deo universos intra sanctam ecclesiam catholicam et apostolicam servire volentes et omnes sequentes ordines: sacerdotes, diaconos, subdiaconos, acolythos, exorcistas, lectores, ostiarios et omnes clericos, universos religiosos et religiosas, omnes pueros et parvulos et parvulas, pauperes et egenos, reges et principes, laboratores et agricolas, servos et dominos, omnes virgines et continentes et maritatas, laicos, masculos et feminas, omnes infantes, adolescentes, iuvenes et senes, sanos et infirmos, omnes pusillos et magnos, et omnes

populos, gentes, tribus et linguas, omnes nationes et omnes homines ubicumque terrarum, qui sunt et erunt.[36]

This is a remarkable passage that brings together all sorts of classifications of diverse principles and origins, that gives dignity to some from the undervalued categories, and encompasses the whole earth and all time to come. However, the text erases social antagonisms and addresses secular society with all the ambiguity of an attitude that embraces, but also drowns, the social structures in a uniform fraternity. The strength and draw of the appeal can be imagined, but also the disappointment for the medieval masses that the concept contains.

But it was indeed the masses, all classes and all genders mixed, who hastened to see Francis and to drink in his words. The expressions repeated in the writings of his biographers are significant: 'populus' ('the people'), 'magnus populus' ('the great mass'), 'multi di populo' ('many members of the common people'), 'nobiles et ignobiles' ('noblemen and commoners'), 'clerici et laici' ('clergy and laity'), 'non solum viri sed etiam virgines et viduae' ('not only men but also many virgins and widows'), 'cunctus populus' ('the entire people'), 'parvi et magni' ('the small and the great'), 'homines et mulieres' ('men and women'), etc.

The laity

Franciscanism was both part of a religious movement to promote the laity inside Christianity and part of a general movement for the 'secularisation' of society. Georges de Lagarde is the historian of the ideas and theories involved in these developments.[37]

When the Order first began, the *Regula bullata*, in chapter three, ratifies the presence of *laici* beside *clerici*. John Mundy has noted that the Mendicants, especially the Franciscans, brought about a radical change in the condition of the lay brothers in relation to the monastic structures and traditions. They belonged to the First Order, while the lay men and women who stayed in the world comprised the Third Order. In the early days, the Third Order was better able to 'set the tone in the brothers' homes', because the brother priests were more concerned with the apostolate in the outside world.[38]

An example of a lay person in the early days of the Order is John Iwyn, a burgher and haberdasher of London, who was noted for his piety, 'having entered as a layman into the religious life, he left us the example of perfect penance and the highest devotion' ('ipse ut laicus ingressus religionem perfectissime penitentiae et summae devotionis nobis exempla reliquit').[39]

In this regard, the general chapter of Rome of 1239 turned a decisive page and suppressed a remarkable experiment, when, despite providing for some extremely rare exceptions, it in fact excluded the laity from the Order. Raoul Manselli has clearly shown the process of clericalisation of the Order in the thirteenth century, a decisive phenomenon that re-established the frontier of clericalism between the brothers and the laity.[40]

Women

Saint Francis and thirteenth-century Franciscanism allowed a place for women to a degree and in a perspective unparalleled in any other religious milieu of the time – except, of course, among the Beguines and the great Benedictine mystics of Helfta at the end of the century.

For Saint Francis, woman appears as a dream image and has the value of a symbol. Francis 'seeks a spouse' and 'dreams of his lady'. Besides the spouse and the lady, the mother is also a frequent symbol for him. He compared himself to a 'beautiful woman' ('mulier formosa') (*Vita secunda*, 16, 10).[41] Three women luminously crossed the religious life of Francis: Clare of Assisi, Giacoma di Settesoli and, to a lesser extent, Praxede, the Roman recluse.

Saint Clare brought the founding of the Second Order, the Poor Ladies, in close association with the First, the men's order.

In his first letter of 1216, Jacques de Vitry commented on the women in the movement. He wrote,

> I have found consolation in seeing a great number of men and women who gave up all their possessions and left the world for the love of Christ: 'minor brothers' and 'minor sisters', so are they named . . . The women occupy hospices and refuges near the different towns; they live there in community from their own manual labour, without accepting any revenue.

And he also commented: 'The reverence that clerics and lay people show the women is a burden to them; it aggrieves and annoys them.'[42]

It should be recalled that in his letters Francis made a point of addressing both the men and the women, and that his biographers emphasised how many women were in his audiences.

The close connections of the Franciscans with many confraternities of the Virgin have been noted. According to Giovanni Miccoli's brilliant clarification of the function of Marian devotion among the faithful, in particular the laity, it offers a particularly effective mediation for approaching the divinity, an approach which is easier than liturgical and iconographical esotericism.[43]

However, the presence of women and of femininity among the Minors had another side to it. Francis and his brothers shared the Christian and more specifically monastic tradition of the woman temptress who must be avoided. Chapter twelve of the *Regula non bullata* calls on the brothers to keep away 'from the evil aspect and the frequenting of women' ('a malo visu et frequentia mulierum'). Chapter eleven of the *Regula bullata* forbids them 'to visit or take counsel from women' ('suspecta consortia vel consilia mulierum') or to enter monasteries of cloistered nuns.

If marriage was not an obstacle to belonging to the Third Order, it was an obstacle to entering the first. Sexual abstinence, which the Gregorian reform made one of the principal features differentiating the clergy from the laity, was imposed on the brothers by the *Regula bullata*. The second chapter, which specifies the conditions of admission, stipulates that married postulants will not be admitted and that exceptions will be made only for those whose wife has already entered a monastery or has allowed them, with the approval of the diocesan bishop, to enter into religious life, having taken a vow of chastity herself, and being, by her age, above suspicion. Thus, the boundary of marriage that separated the clergy from the laity passed between the brothers and the laity, and woman remained an ambiguous and a dangerous being.[44]

Children

In an era that paid scant attention to children, Francis and the Minors are part of the lineage which increased the value placed on children. Its other main representatives were Saint Bernard, almost a century earlier, and Jacques de Vitry, a contemporary (and supporter) of the first Franciscans, who includes a category of 'pueri' in his *Sermones ad status*.

Children appear twice in the categories of Christians in the *Regula non bullata* (XXII, 7): first among the dominated,[45] and then among the age groups: 'infantes', 'adolescentes', 'iuvenes' and 'senes'. A popular episode, the 'crib' scene of Greccio, contributed to spreading the cult of baby Jesus, which played a role in the advancement of children comparable to the cult of the Virgin for women.[46]

Charity

I will not dwell on this attitude that is well known. It is founded on love. God is love, 'Deus est caritas'. In the *Laudes Dei altissimi*, attributed to Brother Leo, God is defined as love and 'charity': '*Tu es amor, caritas*', and certain manuscripts repeat at the end of these lauds: '*tu es caritas nostra*', in an enumeration of the three theological virtues. In the *Regula non bullata* on two occasions (XVII, 5; XXII, 26) Francis refers to the first Epistle of John (chapter 4) who declares that God is love ('Deus caritas est'), that his love for us is perfect ('perfecta est caritas Dei nobiscum'), and that if we love God we must by the same token love our neighbour ('qui diligit Deum, diligat et fratrem suum'). The love that God has for us and that we must have for him is also for Francis the foundation of love for one's neighbour, and he repeats it on many occasions.[47] For example, in the 'Second Letter to the Faithful' (30–1) he states: 'habemus itaque caritatem' and immediately adds 'et faciamus eleemosynas' ('we therefore have love and must give charity'). This whole paragraph is also permeated with *misericordia*.

More directly related to the purpose of this chapter is the fact that this proclamation of the love of God and of one's neighbour in the thirteenth century generated institutions and practices in which the Franciscans (and the other Mendicants) fell in with a more general trend.

As early as the turn of the thirteenth century, there were 'rich Italian merchants beginning to do charitable works on a grand scale'.[48] They founded *case di misericordia*, hospitals.

Now, in Florence for example, the first Minors asked for hospitality at the hospital of San Gallo, founded in 1218, while in 1219 the Preachers asked for it at the hospital of San Pancrazio.

Franciscans and other Mendicants played a major role in perfecting and practising the new system of charity: *works of compassion*. The Franciscans were interested more especially in the poor and the sick. A specific instance was the care they gave to *lepers*, by which Francis and his companions demonstrated, as Giovanni Miccoli has well perceived, their desire to challenge established values.[49]

Models related to the structure of religious society

Prelacy

Francis always respected the priesthood and the church hierarchy. He reminded his brothers in the testament of Siena 'always to be faithful and obedient to the prelates and all the clergy of Holy Mother Church' ('ut semper praelatis et omnibus clericis sanctae matris ecclesiae fideles et subjecti existant').

He accepted prelates into the Order and even praised perfect obedience. But should a prelate order a brother to do something *contra animam*, the latter had the right not to obey, without thereby breaking with the superior (and hence the convent and perhaps the Order). Prelates were not to boast of their prelacy, but fulfil it as though it were a matter of washing the brothers' feet (*Admonitions*, 3 and 4).

Francis, however, refused the prelacy for himself (*Vita secunda*, 138, and *Speculum perfectionis*, 43, at the same time as Saint Dominic did). He saw in the prelacy 'an opportunity to fall' (*Vita secunda*, 145). He was suspicious of 'power'.

He detested everything 'superior', everything defined by particles of superiority: *magis-* (*magnus, magister, magnatus*), *prae-* (*praelatus, prior*), *super-* (*superior, superbus*). The people that he wanted to exalt were those undervalued by society: *minores, subditi*. What he desired in his order was *uniformitas*, equality (*Vita secunda*, 191).[50]

This tendency corresponded to a broad contemporary movement in secular society and the struggle against *superbia*. This was the sin of the nobles, the supreme feudal sin, and, perhaps even more so, of church society where criticism of the prelates – no doubt partly under the influence of the heretics and to remove from them an argument against the Church – became more lively than ever.[51]

Fraternity

Francis did not want to be a monk – he went out into human society. If the curia had not forced it on him, he would not have had his disciples form an Order. His ideals of uniformity and equality, on the one hand, and of love, on the other, led him to adopt the term 'brother' or 'friar' for himself and his companions – what was to become his Order he had conceived of as a *fraternitas*.

This term had at that time powerful resonance and connotations. It opposed the Minors (and the other Mendicants) to the monks and the canons. Pierre Michaud-Quantin has highlighted the disappearance of the term *congregatio* from the vocabulary of the Mendicants, following the suppression of institutional and permanent ties between the religious and the house where he resided, ties such as those expressed by the vow of monastic stability.[52]

However, *fraternity* was also in contrast to *consortium*, a vague word more or less equivalent of *universitas*, but whose meaning was changing in the thirteenth century from one emphasising the institutional aspect of the collectivity to one emphasising the internal connections among its members.[53] The secular masters of the school of theology of the University of Paris formed a *consortium*, and this institution that emphasised *function* and *common interests* did much to intensify the conflict with the masters of the Mendicant Orders during the period 1250–9.

Fraternitas, with its doublet *confraternitas*, is above all a name for *confraternity*, the religious counterpart of the corporation, which was at the very heart of the great movement of association characteristic of thirteenth-century urban society. And it is a term in which we find again the overtones of *caritas* where love, fraternity and charity are intimately blended.[54]

Fraternity also makes allusion to the first Christian community of Jerusalem, and the emphasis placed on the core coexistence of the clergy and the laity.

It is, finally, a way to define the future order as a *family*, a concept dear to Francis, and that is also expressed in other family relationships, for instance and above all, the mother–son relationships that are underscored in 'A Rule for Hermitages', in which they are also introduced as a model of fraternity in the feminine, through reference to Martha and Mary. The importance of a code of family relationships to define the community, and then the Franciscan Order, deserves closer examination at a time when medievalists are taking increasing interest in the interconnections of family relationships and created relationships.[55]

Models related to culture in a narrow sense

Intellectual work

Saint Francis's attitude to knowledge and intellectual work was predominantly one of suspicion, if not hostility. I perceive three motivations and three essential aspects of this distrust: the current concept of knowledge as treasure, which clashed with his sense of bare simplicity; the need to own books, objects at that time expensive and seemingly luxurious, which went against his desire for poverty and non-possession; and knowledge as a source of pride and dominance, of intellectual power, which contradicted the vocation of humility.

The supporting texts are many. For example, the renunciation of the possession and the ownership of knowledge are explicitly presented here as a condition of admittance into the Order:

> a great cleric must renounce even knowledge when he enters the Order, so that, freed of this possession, he can offer himself naked in the arms of the Crucifix.
>
> (magnum clericum etiam scientiae quodam modo resignare debere, cum veniret ad Ordinem, ut tali expropriatus possessione, nudum se offeret brachiis Crucifixi.)
>
> (*Vita secunda*, 192)

And in the well-known passage in the *Fioretti*, 8, Francis says to Brother Leo that perfect joy for a Minor does not consist in knowing all the languages and all the sciences and all the writings, in speaking the language of the angels, in knowing the course of the stars and the benefits of herbs, in knowing all the treasures of the earth, the virtues of the birds and fish, of all the animals and of men, of trees and stones, and of roots and waters. Certainly, this text is less an attack on knowledge than a call to joy 'in the cross of tribulation and affection'. It remains that Francis particularly emphasised the dangers of pride in connection with knowledge and learning.

Here, he was going against the current of his times, of the development of a Christianity that needed knowledge to fight heresy, to govern the Church and, simply, to satisfy a mental need, to achieve a Christian humanism in which knowledge has its share.

Francis, however, made concessions and if, in the Rules, he strictly limited the possession of books (*Regula non bullata*, III) and accepted the illiterate into the Order without any obligation to study (*Regula bullata*, X, 8), in practice he revered the learned and consulted them.[56] In his *Testament*, not only did he want the manuscripts 'containing the words of the Lord' to be placed in a more dignified location, but he prescribed that the brothers should honour and revere the theologians 'who provide us with spirit and life' ('sicut qui ministrant nobis spiritum et vitam').

In truth, the Order was quickly to give learning an ever greater place in connection with university teaching.[57] The essential stages in this process were the bull *Ordinem vestrum* of Innocent IV, which would practically exclude the illiterate from the Order; then the generalship of John of Parma (1247–57) who said that the building of the Order rested on two walls, 'namely, good morals and knowledge' ('scilicet moribus bonis et scientia'), and emphasised that 'the brothers must raise the wall of knowledge beyond the heavens to seek God' ('parietem scientiae fecerunt fratres ultra coelos et coelestia sublimem, in tantum ut quaererunt, an Deus sit');[58] and, finally, during Saint Bonaventure's office as minister general from 1257 to his death in 1274.[59]

Bonaventure definitively made the possession of books part of the very nature of the Order:

> The Rule imperatively requires the brothers to fulfil the authority and office of preaching, in such terms as are not found, I believe, in any other Rule. Therefore if they are not to preach nonsense but divine words instead, they cannot know these if they do not read: they cannot read if they have no books; it is thus very clear that having books is part of the perfection of the Rule in the same way as preaching.
>
> (*Epistola de tribus questionibus*)

Now far from considering knowledge and books as a monopoly of the clergy, he considered them as instruments in the service of evangelisation, and he recommended the brothers to write books of popularisation for the use of the laity.

Finally, with the examples of Roger Bacon and Raymond Lull, there was no longer any contradiction between total knowledge and the most fervent Franciscan spirituality.

The spoken word

The advance of books and writing in the Order only served to enrich the spoken word. Here the Franciscans remained very close to secular society, where the spoken word predominated to an overwhelming extent within an audiovisual culture in which the *image* should also be studied (a task of which I am incapable).

The spoken word was, of course, essentially that of preaching. This for Francis had the aim of transmitting the words of Jesus Christ, who is the Word of the Father and the words of the Holy Ghost that are Spirit and Life (Letter 1, 'First Letter to the Faithful'). In Letter 2, 'Second Letter to the Clergy', Francis even went so far as to put the words of Jesus on the same plane as his body and his blood. There is thus a Franciscan theology of the word.

In the bull *Solet annuere* of 29 September 1223, approving the Rule of the Minors, Honorius III assigned to Franciscan preaching goals that were more modest.

> In their preaching may their words be chaste and judicious, showing the people the vices and the virtues, the pains of hell and the glory of paradise, in short sermons, for the Lord spoke over the earth with a brief verb.
> (In praedicatione quam faciunt sint casta et examinata eorum eloquia, ad utilitatem et aedificationem populi, annuntiando eis vitia et virtutes, poenam et gloriam, cum brevitate sermonis, quia verbum abbreviatum fecit Dominus super terram.)[60]

This recommendation of brevity in preaching may have been inspired by the desire to prevent Francis and the brothers from yielding to the temptation to give marathon sermons. However, the Pope was probably thinking especially of church sermons, at Mass, where brevity, it seems, was indeed appreciated by the congregations,[61] while the Franciscans had a liking for preaching out of doors, addressing crowds and able to continue for a long time.

The Minors knew how to use certain new forms of speech[62] that instituted new types of relationships – less distant, less hierarchical than in the past.

According to Thomas of Spalato, who heard him in Bologna on 15 August 1222, 'his speeches did not issue from the grand style of sacred eloquence; instead they were more like harangues',[63] and *The Legend of the Three Companions* also insists on the fact that Francis spoke the language of sincerity more than that of rhetoric.[64]

We know that the Franciscans, like the other Mendicants, made great use of *exempla* in their sermons and were among the first authors of collections of *exempla*. These moralising little stories were appropriate to the nature of their preaching, by introducing precisely this atmosphere of daily life and this air of living truth, of direct testimony, which corresponded to their style and to the literary genre of the *exemplum*.[65]

It is necessary finally to note the use of the spoken word in two particular cases involving important phenomena of the thirteenth century: the crusade and the anti-heretical struggle.

In both situations, Francis had hoped that the struggle could be accomplished through the spoken word and through example and could result in the conversion of the infidels and the heretics. In the case of the crusade, Davide Bigalli has shown how Roger Bacon, making use of Aristotle, defined the spoken word, the *verbum*, as a power, a *potestas*. The *sermo potens* ('power of the word') is, in this respect, different from power rooted in the truth of faith. Thus, finding inspiration again in Saint Francis, Roger Bacon placed the spoken word in the centre of the 'universal *christificatio*' and replaced the crusade in a theology of the spoken word and of the cross of Christ.[66]

As for heresy, *persuasio* slid into *coercitio*.[67] It was first the perversion of the word, and then the renunciation of the use of words of persuasion that was to lead to the acceptance by the Minors of the anti-heretical struggle in Italy (1254) and to the end of the history of the *fraternitas* of Saint Francis. Raoul Manselli has given a thoughtful account of this.

The vernacular language

Sermons had long been given liberally to the laity in the vernacular language. Nevertheless, the impact of the Mendicants and the Franciscans, in particular, on the promotion of the vernacular languages was significant. Indeed, they appeared and equalised much of Western Christian society in this thirteenth century that saw the affirmation of the vernacular languages in literature and in the chancelleries, where the movement to translate Latin into vernacular languages grew rapidly.[68] Only a few particularly striking points will be emphasised.

We know the major significance to the history of Italian poetry of Saint Francis with the 'Cantico di Frate Sole' and of Jacopone da Todi with his *Laude*. Secular communities of *laudesi* developed and popularised this form of sung poetry. It has been advanced that the Mendicant brothers and, especially, the Franciscans, with their actions and gestures, made possible the development of the theatre and its independence from liturgy.[69] Let us remember that Saint Francis sang the praises of God in French and liked to sing in French when his soul was overflowing with joy.

Raymond Lull has been considered the 'creator of Catalan'.

However, the Friars Minor were not fanatical about the use of the vernacular language as a means of communication. According to Thomas of Eccleston, for example, Peter of Tewksbury, minister of the Franciscan province of England, had six or seven foreign clerics come, 'who, not knowing English, would preach by example' ('qui scilicet, quamvis nescirent Anglicum, exemplo praedicarent').[70]

Arithmetic

Alexander Murray has drawn attention to the emergence of an 'arithmetical mentality' in the thirteenth century. Among the examples that he cites is that of Salimbene's milieu. Salimbene, he remarks, was familiar with numbers. He made note of the year, the month and the day. He gave nine lists of prices of foodstuffs. He quoted figures for battles, for expenses and for distances, and tried to make them accurate. After the maritime defeat of the Pisans by the Genoans, in 1284, he wondered: how many dead and wounded? However, he did not trust the figure provided by the archbishop of Pisa. 'I have decided', he wrote, 'to wait for the Minors of Genoa and Pisa to furnish a more reliable number.' The Franciscans' taste for numerical precision is thus evoked, and Alexander Murray concludes: 'Salimbene and his brothers were pioneers.' They were pioneers of arithmetic.[71]

Models of behaviour and sensibility

Courtesy

Besides the religious models, those of monasticism and saintliness in particular, in the medieval Christian West there were secular cultural models, including the 'aristocratic' models which Georges Duby has made his special focus of study.[72]

At the end of the twelfth century, the secular society of the aristocracy and chivalry produced the first systematic code of secular values: courtesy.

This code attracted Francis in his youth. No doubt he took it in along with his French culture, and the fascination that the knightly life and culture held for him echoes in his biographies.

The most surprising fact is that this taste and this style continued at least partially after his conversion. His love of poverty was expressed through the symbolism and the vocabulary of courtly love. It was 'Lady Poverty'. He kept his greatness of soul, his 'magnanimitas' (*Vita prima*, 4, 13; 13, 11; *Vita secunda*, 3, 14), and he remained very courteous, 'curialissimus' (*Vita prima*, 17, 15; *Vita secunda*, 3).[73]

However, he put his ideal of chivalry in the service of Christ and of the Church.

The dream of the palace filled with weapons (*Vita prima*, 5; *Vita secunda*, 5, 6; *Legenda minor*, 1, 3) certainly marked his renunciation of the chivalrous life, but it revealed how deeply this mode of feeling and self-expression had affected him.

In my view, Giovanni Miccoli has underestimated the implications of the texts in which Francis cries to a group of brigands, 'I am the herald of the great King' (*Vita prima*, 16), or declares, 'Here are my knights of the Round Table, the brothers who are hiding away in distant and lonely places to devote themselves to prayer and meditation' (*Leg. Per.*, 71). Or again, Francis replied to a novice who was asking for a psalter:

> The emperor Charles, Roland and Oliver, and all the paladins and pious warriors who were mighty in combat, pursued the infidels until death, sparing neither sweat nor fatigue, and won a memorable victory over them; and to finish, these martyr saints died while fighting for the faith of Christ. Now

we see many who would like to bring honour and glory on themselves by merely singing about their exploits.

(*Leg. Per.*, 72)

For Miccoli, these statements do not represent anything substantial in the religious experience of Francis.[74] However, he does add very perceptively that these expressions show Francis's capacity 'to communicate and express himself in the current language, through images and references known to everyone, outside the channels and traditional meditations of religious and moral literature'.[75]

Here, indeed, was a language that brought Francis closer to the laity. Nevertheless, I think that the courtly vocabulary of Francis was not just a means to take part in the cultural fashions of his secular contemporaries. He was expressing the interiorisation of the warrior heroism that characterised the religiosity of his time. The saint of the high Middle Ages was God's *athlete*; the saint of the thirteenth century was God's *knight*. Here, as in other cultural attitudes, Francis and the Mendicants appeared as the continuators of Saint Bernard and the Cistercians.

This courtly sensibility, this chivalrous attitude, particularly towards Poverty, would persist among the Minors. Jacopone da Todi would say in *Lauda* 59, 'By the love of poverty your seigneurial power is great' ('Povertate ennamorata, grann'è la tua segnoria').[76]

Beauty

Even more than woman, for Francis and the Franciscans, beauty had two faces. On the one hand, it was the highest expression of divine creation. An old and controversial thesis, that of Thode, which makes Franciscanism the father of the Renaissance and of the sense of beauty, has been taken up again more recently by Raffaello Morghen, who also sees in the art of the Minors (single-naved architecture, cycles of frescos) an art of the gentle way of life. Morghen picks up a sentence by Luigi Salvatorelli focusing on the freshness of the aesthetic sensibility of Saint Francis: 'The love of Saint Francis for all creation represents something really and radically new. And the direct sensing of the divine presence in all things is the very perception, filled with enthusiasm, of beauty conferred on the love of God.'[77]

Here again, this sensibility must be put back in its divine, theological foundation.

The Lord is Beauty, as Francis says in the *Laudes Dei altissimi* given to brother Leo, '*Tu es pulchritudo*' (repeated). And the sun, in the 'Canticle of the Creatures', is the symbol of this beauty: '*Et ellu è bellu*' ('And he is beautiful').

Francis compared himself, as we have seen, to a beautiful woman ('mulier formosa') whose sons are very handsome ('filii venustissimi') (*Vita secunda*, 16, 10).

But beauty weakens the will: 'The beauty of the place that can greatly corrupt the vigour of the heart' ('loci amoenitas quae ad corrumpendum animi vigorem non mediocriter potest') (*Vita prima*, 5, 71). The conversion of Francis distanced him from enjoyment of beauty: 'The beauty of the Fields, the pleasure of the vines and everything that is beautiful to the eyes can in no way delight him' ('sed pulchritudo agrorum, vinearum amoenitas et quidquid visu pulchrum est, in nullo potuit eum delectare') (*Vita prima*, 3, 12).

This was indeed the attitude of the thirteenth century that was discovering, attracted but hesitant, a sense of beauty and, in particular, the beauty of the world.[77]

Joy

Pleasure in the world is demonstrated even more clearly in joyful behaviour. Here again, there is a relationship between religious and lay people, while the monastic model made monks the specialists of tears ('is qui luget'). On the contrary, a great many texts show Francis 'hilaris, hilari vultu'.[78]

In his story of the first Minors in England, Thomas of Eccleston supplies repeated testimony of the gaiety of the brothers, which sometimes even appears either forced or excessive.

When the brothers settled in a house in Canterbury, they used to come home in the evening, make a fire, sit around it, cook up some gruel ('potus') in a cauldron and drink it in a circle. It was sometimes so thick that they had to add water to it, but they drank joyfully ('et sic cum gaudio biberunt'). Similarly, at Sarum, in front of the kitchen fire the brothers drank a disgusting brew ('faeces') with so much pleasure and joy ('cum tanta jocundate et laetitia') that they amused themselves by stealing each other's in a friendly way.[79]

At Oxford, the young brothers were so much in the habit of being 'jocundi et laeti' among themselves that just looking at each other made it hard for them not to burst out laughing ('ut vix in aspectu mutuo se temperarent a risu'). These fits of giggles resulted in beatings that were to no effect. A miracle was necessary for the epidemic of laughter to cease.[80]

As for Peter of Tewksbury, he said to a brother,

> Three things are necessary for temporal salvation: food, sleep and play. He ordered a melancholy brother to drink a chalice filled with an excellent wine as a penance. And when he had drunk it, albeit unwillingly, Peter said to him, 'My very dear brother, if you often had such a penance, you would always have a better conscience.'[81]

Francis's motto was 'paupertas cum laetitia' (*Admonitions*, XXVII, 3): poverty in joy.

Indeed, the source of this joy is also of a divine order. It is a transcendent experience, a sign of grace, the effect of the Holy Ghost; is it born of the discovery of the Gospels and of poverty. The Devil can do nothing against it (*Vita secunda*, 88).

Finally, joy combines with asceticism and the experience of pain to be consummated in love. Bonaventure describes it in the *De triplici via*:

> This path begins under the spur of conscience and finishes with the feeling of spiritual joy; it is exercised in pain, but is consummated in love.
> (incipit via ista a stimulo conscientiae et terminatur ad affectum spiritualis laetitiae, et exercetur in dolore, sed consummatur in amore.)

Death

This joyful spirituality did not prevent the Franciscans from making the thought of death part of their daily practice. Ideas of death also took on new forms, both individual (the importance of individual judgment and purgatory) and collective (funeral preparations and practices of the brothers) in the thirteenth century.

The following features can be identified in the Franciscan spirituality of death which, in its turn, influenced that of the laity. It involved, first, devotion to the *dead* Christ, to the Passion, which pervades the episode of the stigmata of Saint Francis; second, the brothers' zeal in praying for their deceased brothers. It also involved the receiving of dead lay people into the convents and churches of the Order, a practice for which the papacy gave the Franciscans permission only in 1250, although it had been granted to the Dominicans as early as 1227.

It was finally – in the 'The Canticle of the Creatures' – 'our Sister Bodily Death, from whom no one living can escape', which is not to be feared, because only the 'second death', damnation, is terrible.

Ethical and religious models in the strict sense

These are the most widely known and, despite their significance, I will not dwell on them.

Penance

The thirteenth century was an age of penitents,[82] and the Franciscan movement was a movement of penance, and as such very much part of the society of its time.[83]

The *Legenda trium sociorum* (34) presents Francis as a pioneer in this area: 'The way of penance was then completely unknown and considered folly.' In the *Testament*, he presents his conversion as a conversion to penance: 'The Lord gave to me, Brother Francis, the task of beginning penance' ('Dominus ita dedit mihi fratri Francisco incipere faciendi poenitentiam').

Francis and his brothers adapted the penitential life to the laity while taking into account, as stated above, what appears to have been the great obstacle on the path of penance for the laity: marriage. Laymen would ask them, 'We have wives whom we cannot leave behind. Teach us which path of salvation we can take.'

Confession is a prerequisite of penance. And the Minors, like the Preachers, favoured the practice of annual confession decreed in the canon *Omnis utriusque sexus* of Lateran IV (1215). They composed manuals for confessors and became specialists in the theory and practice of confession.

The search for intention and the practice of confession audible only to the confessor, led to an emphasis on *admission*. The thirteenth century saw the advent of admission both in its liberating and in its inquisitorial forms (torture). 'Blessed is he who admits humbly', says Francis ('Beatus . . . qui humiliter confitetur') (*Admonitions*, XXII).

Poverty

Two questions should shed light on Franciscan poverty: 'Is Franciscan poverty a continuity or a discontinuity in relation to earlier concepts and practices?' 'What relationships did the voluntary poverty of the Franciscans maintain with the involuntary poor of the thirteenth century and what is the significance of the expression *sicut alii pauperes* (*Regula non bullata*, II, 7–8)?'. The first of these has been fully treated,[84] but the second has been the subject of preliminary works only.[85] It is nevertheless vital from a historical as well as a theoretical point of view.

Humility[86]

Its model is obviously the humility of Jesus. It is the sister of poverty.

Begging, its specifically Franciscan incarnation (also, to a lesser degree, Dominican and practised by other thirteenth-century Orders known as 'Mendicant'), poses a substantial historical problem. Begging was not in the tradition of Western monasticism and was explicitly forbidden to the clergy. It was practised but only marginally by wandering preachers at the turn of the eleventh to the twelfth century, and the Rule of Grandmont welcomed it as an 'exercise in asceticism and humility'.[87] Here again, it must be situated in the history of a long-enduring character: the beggar.

For the socio-political aspects – prohibition of civil duties to the brothers, mistrust of the prelates, the ideal of equality, and the ideology of inferiority (*minors*) – see the passages above on the models related to the structure of global (civil) and religious society.[88]

Purity and the body

In his love for the whole of creation, Francis makes one exception: the body, which must be hated ('First Letter to the Faithful'). The flesh is a barrier separating us from God (*Vita prima*, 15). Certainly, contemptible as it is, the body (*Regula non bullata*, XXIII, 23–24) is a gift from God, and for this it must be loved. And Francis even says (*Admonitions*, V) that God created man in the image of his beloved Son in the body, while he created him in His own likeness in the soul (which refers to the Christic Passion and its imitation as the finality of the body). Certainly, there is mention of 'brother body' in 'The Canticle of the Creatures' and Thomas of Celano reports a talk by Francis on how to care for the body (*Vita secunda*, 160). But the body is the source of sin (*Regula non bullata*, XXII, 5), so it must be despised and hated.[89]

However, rather than the opposition lust/chastity, the true Franciscan opposition is flesh/purity, which includes more than the body and encompasses the heart and the mind. The seven deadly sins – of which lust is one – seem to have little prominence in the thought of Saint Francis and perhaps in thirteenth-century Franciscanism. In a general way, the action of Francis (and the Franciscans) was often done by displacement of values and practices.

Purity is the neighbour of simplicity. Purity is a divine quality that only God possesses entirely. We can distinguish a purity of the senses, a purity of the heart, and a purity of the mind. In the symbolic spirituality of the four elements of 'The Canticle of the Creatures', it is water, 'our sister water', that incarnates purity; she is said to be chaste and humble, too. Purity belongs to that great nebula of Franciscan values in which humility is the centre of gravity.

In chapter five of *De adventu fratrum minorum in Angliam*, Thomas of Eccleston discusses 'the primeval purity of the brothers' ('de primitiva puritatae fratrum'). This purity, that was also called 'simplicitas', was especially marked by 'castitas' (nocturnal pollutions had to be confessed publicly), and by 'laetitia' and 'hilaritas', the gaiety mentioned above.

On attitudes to the body, the original Franciscanism clearly diverged from what seems to have been a new general attitude to the body, to the flesh, which, far from being a site of poverty as Francis would have had it, was tending rather to be a site of enjoyment – as evidenced by the spread of aesthetic *nudes* in art (sculpture) and the rise of gastronomy. Francis, who found no trace of alimentary asceticism in the Gospels, supported a moderate position. Let us recall the anecdote of Giordano di Giano: Francis was eating meat with Peter Catani. Along came a brother with the new constitutions of the Order that forbade eating meat. Saint Francis's reaction was, 'Let us eat, as the Gospels teach, what is put before us' ('Mangiamo, come insegna il Vangelo, cio che ci viene messo davanti').

Prayer

I do not know of any specific studies on the practice of prayer in original Franciscanism or of its relationships with contemporary practice among the clergy and laity.[90] The question of the balance between very private forms of prayer and the practice (among the Minors also) of a quasi-automatic form of prayer, almost magical, in particular for the *Ave* and the *Pater*, is a matter for speculation.

Saintliness

André Vauchez has brilliantly demonstrated the significant role played by the Mendicants and, notably, the Franciscans in the development of the concept of saintliness with the establishment of an 'evangelical' model (end twelfth–end thirteenth century), founded on asceticism, poverty and pastoral zeal.[91]

For the Franciscans, miracles do not constitute sanctity but are its manifestation. The beginning of the *Legenda trium sociorum* is characteristic in this regard:

> Not satisfied with merely talking about the miracles that reveal saintliness but do not comprise it, but also wanting to show the signs of his holy behaviour and his will to fulfil his pious enjoyment in singing the praises and the glory of almighty God and of the very holy father, and for the enlightenment of those wishing to follow in his footsteps.[92]

A person's life and virtues are what matter.

The appeal of Saint Francis, during his lifetime and after his death, has done much to establish a model of saintliness in which the imitation of Christ plays a large part, and in which humility, poverty and simplicity predominate. But, as we will see below, popular devotion to the Franciscan saints kept the traditional forms, saw them as miracle workers and laid great emphasis on relics.

Traditional models of the sacred

Dreams and visions

Medieval texts are full of dreams and visions. However, the history of dreams and their interpretation in the Middle Ages is little known. It seems that in the thirteenth century dreams were made known widely, including those of the poor. Previously only the dreams of the great had been recorded (in continuation of the ancient theme of the *royal dream*) as well as those of the saints, who were particularly subject to dreams interpreted as temptation by the Devil or as special divine visions.[93]

A study dedicated to his dreams concludes that Saint Francis had rather fewer than other saints.[94] Nevertheless, at least three groups of significant dreams can be distinguished:

1   the dreams and visions connected with the conversion of Saint Francis, reported by Thomas of Celano, Bonaventure and *The Legend of the Three Companions*.[95] These are the dreams or visions of Saint Francis himself (including the famous dream about weapons),[96] of the bishop of Assisi and of Pope Innocent III. These last are rather traditional;
2   the eighteen visions recorded by Thomas of Eccleston in his *De adventu fratrum minorum in Angliam*;
3   the visions of Brother Giles, in the manner of the *Fioretti*.

This list suffices to show that the dream/vision was one of the favourite methods of exposition in Franciscan society. It also represents a lived experience that deserves further study.

Miracles, witchcraft and exorcism

While miracles do not constitute saintliness in the view of the first Minors, the Franciscan miracles, those of Saint Francis and Saint Anthony of Padua, enjoyed a great vogue, either because they were seen as a re-enactment of miracles of Christ, or because they expressed the persistence, if not the intensification, of the traditional attitudes of the medieval masses to miracles.

All the biographies of Saint Francis mention his miracles and, according to tradition, Thomas of Celano composed a separate *Treatise on the Miracles* of the saint.

The 'Life of Saint Anthony of Padua' records the explosion of miracles that took place after Saint Francis's death and the crowds of strangers who flocked to his tomb:

There the eyes of the blind were opened; the ears of the deaf were unsealed; the lame began to leap like deer; the tongues of the mute were quickly untied to sing the praises of God. Paralysed limbs regained their former capabilities; hunchback, gout, fever and the various epidemics of illnesses were put to flight . . . the Venetians came running; the Trevisans made haste; the Vicenins arrived, and so did the Lombards, the Slavs, the Aquileans, the Teutons, and the Hungarians. . . .[97]

In a suggestive study, André Goddu has graphed the frequency of the accounts of exorcism in the lives of the saints as related in the *Acta sanctorum* (Paris and Rome, 1866–1940). Goddu has suggested that this curve essentially highlights the efficacy or failure of exorcism.[98] The peak reached in the thirteenth century would thus correspond to a period of difficulties for belief in exorcism. Yet the exorcisms accomplished by Saint Francis and Saint Anthony of Padua were significant.[99]

Bearers of new models and of modernity, the Franciscans comfortably took their place among the old traditions and proven models.

Conclusion

I will not attempt to give a synthetic response to the basic issues to which all historians of Franciscanism contribute before considering the following question: how did the thirteenth-century Franciscans change the attitude of the Church to secular society and the behaviour of the laity itself – in this century when, despite brief bursts of millenarianism, Christianity no longer believed that the end of the world was near and when it became established as an earthly institution?

I will make just three comments.

The Franciscans were the principal disseminators of the idea that an individual does not attain salvation alone, and that it is all humanity, and all creation that must attain salvation. Certainly, monks wanted to be the model for the whole of society and the purpose of their asceticism was not merely their personal salvation, but the salvation of the world through their intercession with God. It remains that the monastic model was that of solitary penance. The Mendicants and especially the Minors preached by word and by example that all humanity must attain salvation through a communal penance whose models are not the top of the hierarchy, but the bottom, among the most humble and the poorest, among lay people as well as the clergy. Certainly, they did not abolish the boundary between clergy and laity, even inside their own Order since the laity were expelled from it at an early date, but they gave a prime impetus to the idea of a community of destiny in which the difference between clergy and laity is set aside.

They strikingly affirmed in their doctrine and behaviour the ambiguity of the world in which they lived. It is, on the one hand, a world created by God that one must love, a source of joy and of total fraternity, but also distorted by the Devil and by sin that must be opposed. This must be rejected uncompromisingly where it appears as an essential source of inequality and enmity, of any form of power, whether founded on property, money and knowledge, or on the power of rank, birth and flesh. It is in this tension between the joyful acceptance of the world and the rejection of its perversion that people must find their salvation, in the dialectic between receptivity and reaction. This was, of course, an ideal, of which the Minors often fell short, even as early as the thirteenth century. An anonymous Tuscan poet of the middle of the century said of them:

> No one wants to see himself poor,
> riches, everyone who can get them,
> has them.
> (Povero nessum non voglion vedere,
> dei richi, tutti quanti ponno avere,
> tutti li ànno.)[100]

Nevertheless, the expression of the ideal and the reference to the ideal remain.[101]

Finally, the Franciscans gave an actual historical model of the new man, a penitent torn and finally crucified, Francis himself, the only character to have played this role in Western Christendom, a Christian modelled on Jesus and following in his footsteps. He did not give rise to a personality cult, whose profoundly perverting nature, whatever its model may be, is well known. He was the personal embodiment of the impulse to community, poorest of the poor, humblest of the humble, who travelled throughout Christendom from the overcrowded cities to the solitudes of nature, from Umbria to Spain and the Holy Land.

Here again, seen from a historical perspective, Franciscanism was rooted in a world that was being organised into communities – this was the great age of corporations, of fraternities, of universities – at the same time as the sense and the affirmation of the individual were developing in it. Despite their troubles, their contradictions, and their failures, the Minors, more than almost any other religious movement, were in close harmony with the spirit of their times, adapting to a new society in its advances and in its denials, expressing in ideological and spiritual terms the transition from feudalism to capitalism, or rather, to use José Luis Romero's expression, the development of a feudal-bourgeois system.

But there are also few other movements so well able to express and to illuminate all periods of human history. To be at once receptive and resistant to the world is a model, a plan for yesterday and today, and no doubt for tomorrow.

And in our own time, our outlook and our efforts must above all be brought to bear on the tragic countries of the Third World and take their lowly, their poor and their oppressed as our model because despite its failures, setbacks and betrayals, the lesson of Franciscanism is still there in its great sweep towards secular society. As long as hunger, misery and oppression are unvanquished, it remains a valuable lesson for our time.

NOTES

2 In search of the true Saint Francis

1 'Ed io con le mie mani lavoravo, come voglio lavorare; e voglio che lavorano tutti gli altri frati, di onesto lavoro.'

2 'A tutte le podestà, a tutti i consoli, giudici e rettori nel mondo intero come a tutti gli altri a cui il documento può pervenire.'

3

La sua famiglia, che si mosse drittu
coi piedi a le sue orme, è tanto volta,
che quel dinanza a quel di retro gitta
E tosto si vedrà de la ricolta
de la mala coltura, quando il loglio
Si lagnerà de l'arca li sia tolta
Ben dico, chi cercasse a foglio a foglio
nostro volume, ancor troveria carta
u'leggerebbe 'I mi son quel ch'i'soglio',
ma non fia da Casal né d'Acquasparta,
là onde vegnon tali a la scrittura,
ch'uno la fugge, e altro la coarta.
(Dante, *Divine Comedy*, *Paradise*, XII, vv. 115–26)

These words, which Dante gives to Saint Bonaventure, deplore the divisions of the family or posterity of Saint Francis. The bad disciples complain they have been excluded, but they have done bad work. Francis must remain what he was, distant from both those who, like the spiritually ardent Albertino da Casale, enforce his rule too rigidly, and those who, like the minister general of the Minors and Cardinal Mateo d'Acquasparta, evade it.

4 'Il ministro generale e tutti gli altri ministri e custodi per obbedienza siano tenuti a non aggiungere e a non togliere nulla a queste parole. Anzi abbiano sempre con sè questo scritto insieme con la Regola, leggano anche queste parole.'

5 Thomas of Celano is our main source for the biography of Francis of Assisi. We will attempt to present his work, ideas and sensibility according to his writings alone, using all the other sources only to outline, in conclusion, the historical character of Saint Francis and the originality of his place among the protagonists of history.

6 'Vi sono molti, i quali, quando fan peccato o ricevono alcun torto, spezzo incolpano il nemico o il prossimo. Ma non è cosi: poichè ognuno ha in suo potere il nemico, cioè il corpo, per mezzo del quale pecca' (*Admonitions*, 10).

7 'Considera, uomo, in quale stato eccellente ti ha messo il Signore, poichè ti ha creato e formato *ad imaginem* del suo Figliolo diletto secondo il corpo, ed a sua somiglianza lo spirito' (*Admonitions*, 5).

8
Il Signore cosi donò a me, frate Francesco, la grazia di cominciare a far penitenza: quando ero ancora nei peccati, mi pareva troppo amaro vedere i lebbrosi, e il Signore stesso mi condusse tra loro e con essi usai misericordia: quando me ne allontanai, quello che prima mi pareva amaro, tosto mi si mutò in dolcezza d'animo e di corpo. Indi attesi poco, e uscii dal mondo.

9
Tutti i frati si guardino dal monstrare alcun potere o superiori specialmente tra loro. Infatti, come dice il Signore nel Vangelo: *I principi delle nazioni le signoreggiano, e i grandi esercitano il potere sovr'esse*; non sara cosi tra i frati, ma *chiunque vovra essere maggiore tra essi sia loro ministro e servo, e chi sarà maggiore tra essi sia come minore*.

10
Cosi ti dico, figlio mio come madre, che tutte le parole che dicemmo per via brevemente raccolgo in questa parola e consiglio; e non è necessario che tu venga ulteriormente a me per consiglio, perchè così io ti ammonisco: 'In qualunque modo ti sembra di meglio piacere al Signore e di seguire i suoi passi e la sua povertà, fatelo con la benedizione di Dio e con la mia obbedienza. Ma se ti è necessario per la tua anima o per tua consolazione, e vuoi, o Leone, venire da me, vieni pure.'

11 Unless the blond hair and blue eyes come from an unfaithful nineteenth-century restoration.

12 Thomas of Spalato, *Monumenta Germaniae Historia*, Hanover, 1892, vol. 29, p. 580.

13
Furono sì potenti gli Ordini loro nuovi che si sono cagione che la disonestà dei prelati e dei capi della religione non la rovini

vivendo ancora poveramente ed avendo tanto credito nelle con-
fessioni con i popoli, e nelle predicazioni ch'ei danno loro a inten-
dere come gli è male a dir male a che sia bene vivere sotto
l'obbedienza loro e se fanno errori la sciarli castigare da Dio; e
cosi quelli fanno il peggio che possono perchè non temono
quella punizione che non veggono e non credono.

(*Discorsi*, III, 1)

The translation is taken from *Machiavelli: the Chief Works and Others*, trans.
A. Gilbert, Durham, DC: Duke University Press, 1965, vol. 1, p. 422.
14 'non debemus majorem utilitatem habere et reputare in pecunia et denariis
quam in lapidibus.'

3 The vocabulary of social categories in Saint Francis of Assisi and his thirteenth-century biographers

1 This chapter only presents an outline of the strictly limited subject defined
in its title. Its purpose, beyond its immediate relevance, is to show the
problematic nature of historical research and of the historical profession
today. Any inquiry, however limited, can only be conducted, and only
be successful, if it starts questioning how far the past, in which its subject
is embedded, constitutes an inclusive whole and how far the set of tools
available to the historian of the present time is complete. Nothing
better illustrates this twofold necessity than the study of words. To each
word is attached the whole world in which it resonates. To make a word
an object of study, the historian must confront it with his own language,
which is connected to its whole contemporary world. When Francis of
Assisi speaks of the poor, we can understand him only by reference to
the whole society of his time in all its complexity; but we only grasp this
through reference to our own culture, and, to continue with this example,
everything that it provides us with under the category 'poor'. Beyond the
differences in the models put forth by the various historical ideologies of
today, our culture shows us the double and contradictory role of the present in the understanding of the past: it reveals and it conceals. To give
only the most striking example, the Council of Vatican II both clarified
and falsified the perspectives on poverty in the history of Christendom.
Taking note of the existence of these embedded complexities is not redu-
cible to saying that 'everything is in everything and vice versa'. This would
amount to negating the existence of knowledge. It indicates the need for a
multi-levelled analysis and a constant, methodical movement to and fro,
between the structures of the past and those of the present, and each
time from the double perspective of 'objective' realities and of 'mental'
realities. This implies a treatment of totalities that only the methods of
structuralism and recourse to electronic machines seem to make possible.
However, the practical possibilities of this type of study are still very

limited. Thus a historian who has produced small-scale work without a computer, like the work offered here, may well feel dissatisfied (cf. the outline that appeared in *Annales. E.S.C.*, 2, 1968, pp. 335–48).

2 In the edition of H. Boehmer, *Analekten zur Geschichte des Franciscus von Assisi*, Tübingen and Leipzig, 1904, 3rd edn 1961.

3 In the great volume X of *Analecta franciscana (Legendae S. Francisci Assisiensis Saec. XIII et XIV conscriptae. I. Saec. XIII)*, 1926–41. Two interesting lists of the key words of Saint Francis, with references, are given in K. Esser and L. Hardick, *Die Schriften des Hl. Franziskus von Assisi*, Werl/W., 1951, and in Fr Willibrod, *Le Message spirituel de saint François d'Assise dans ses écrits*, Blois, 1960. But these lexicons are mainly concerned with terms referring to properly religious concepts. Volume X of *Analecta franciscana* includes a fine index that has been of great use to us, but which shows some gaps: the references for the terms cited are not exhaustive. Certain words are missing which, beyond their usefulness for our inquiry, should in any case have been included in this extensive index; for example, *dives, fidelis, gastaldi, magister, magnates, negociator, rex.*

4 Elsewhere we are trying to define the relations between 'Mendicant apostolate and urban fact in medieval France' in an inquiry whose outline appeared in *Annales. E.S.C.*, 2, 1968, pp. 335–48.

5 On the concept of holiness in the thirteenth–fourteenth centuries and the decisive moment that Saint Francis and mendicant spirituality represent in its development, André Vauchez has written a Diplôme d'Études Supérieures submitted to the faculty of letters and human sciences of Paris (1962, under the direction of M. Mollat); a dissertation presented at the VIth section of the École pratique des hautes études (1964, under the direction of Jacques Le Goff), unpublished; and is now preparing a doctoral thesis. André Vauchez, *La Sainteté en Occident aux derniers siècles du Moyen Âge d'après les procès de canonisation et les documents hagiographiques*, Rome, 1981.

6 On the significance and the rigidity of literary 'genres' in the Middle Ages, see E. R. Curtius, *European Literature and the Latin Middle Ages*, trans. Willard R. Trask, London, 1953; E. Faral, *Les Arts poétiques du XIIe et du XIIIe siècle. Recherches et documents sur la technique littéraire du Moyen Âge*, Paris, 1923; Th.-M. Charland, *Artes praedicandi. Contribution à l'histoire de la rhétorique au Moyen Âge*, Paris and Ottawa, 1936. Most of the excellent publications on the genre of hagiography, however, from the classic work of Fr H. Delehaye (*Les Légendes hagiographiques*, 1st edn, Brussels, 1905; English translation of 3rd edn, *The Legend of the Saints*, trans. Donald Attwater, Dublin, 1998) to F. Graus's remarkable study (*Volk, Herrscher und Heiliger im Reich der Merowinger. Studien zur Hagiographie des frühen Mittelalters*, Prague, 1965), mainly treat the high Middle Ages.

7 The major problem with the language of preaching in the Middle Ages arises even more sharply with the religious Mendicants and, in particular,

the Franciscans. As for Saint Francis, we know from many passages in his biographies that the language of his mystical outpourings was French (which had probably been the language of the songs and courtly poems that were his delight before his conversion). His biographers very rarely allude to the vernacular Italian language (*lingua romana*), the only specific exception being the word *guardiani*, whose current use for *custodes* has been mentioned (cf. *Analecta franciscana*, X, Index). But Saint Francis was the author of the celebrated 'Canticle of the Creatures' (cf. G. Sabatelli, 'Studi recenti sul Cantico di Frate Sole', *Archivum franciscanum historicum*, 51, 1958), which was, surprisingly, not included by the Quaracchi fathers in their edition of the works of Saint Francis (*Opuscula S. Patris Francisci Assisiensis*, 1904; 3rd edn, 1949) precisely because it had been written in the vernacular. This significant breach made by Francis of Assisi in the Latin fabric of medieval clerical literature did not escape E. R. Curtius in the brilliant work cited in note 6 whose subtle analyses only penetrate to the epidermis of culture (p. 39: 'Italian literature begins only towards 1220, with the Canticle to the Sun of Saint Francis of Assisi'). Of the abundant literature on preaching, I refer readers to R. M. Dessi and M. Lauwers (eds), *La Parole du prédicateur (Ve–XVe siècles)*, Nice, 1997.

8 Cf. R. Roques, *L'Univers dionysien. Structure hiérarchique du monde selon le Pseudo-Denys*, Paris, 1954.

9 Cf., for example, on Saint Anselm the remarkable chapter by R. W. Southern, in *Saint Anselm and his Biographers*, Cambridge, 1963, pp. 107–14, 'The Feudal Imagery'.

10 This deliberate confusion seems to be at the root of the ambiguities in the attempts – very honourable in other connections – of present-day 'Franciscan politics', whose main representative must be Giorgio La Pira.

11 Let us quote the exact words of Alain de Lille at the end of the twelfth century: 'Authority has a nose of wax, one can bend it in different directions' ('Auctoritas cereum nasum habet, id est in diversum potest flecti sensum') (*De fide catholica*, I, 30; *Patrologia Latina*, 210, 333).

12 According to H. Boehmer, *Analekten*, pp. 142–4.

13 Cf. J. Chelini, *Le Vocabulaire politique et social dans la correspondance d'Alcuin*, Aix-en-Provence, 1959; W. Ullmann, 'The Bible and Principles of Medieval Government', *Settimane di Studio di Spoleto*, X, 1963.

14

And Jesus went about all Galilee, teaching in their synagogues, and preaching the gospel of the kingdom, and healing all manner of sickness and all manner of disease among the people. . . . And there followed him great multitudes of people from Galilee.

(Et circuibat Jesus totam Galilaeam, docens in synagogis eorum et praedicans evangelium regni, et sanans omnem languorem et omnem infirmitatem in populo. . . . Et secutae sunt eum turbae multae de Galilea.)

(Matt. 4:23–25)

And many of the people, nobles and commoners, clergy and
laity, began to come to Saint Francis.
(Coeperunt multi de populo, nobiles et ignobiles, clerici et laici .
. . ad sanctum Franciscum accedere.)

(*Vita prima*, 37, p. 30)

Father Francis, having left the secular crowds, who hastened to
him with great devotion every day to hear and see him.
(Pater Franciscus, relictis saecularibus turbis, quae ad audien-
dum et videndum eum quotidie devotissime concurrebant.)

(*Vita prima*, 91, p. 69)

15 The most serious study is that of G. Cambell, 'Les écrits de saint François
d'Assise devant la critique', *Franziskanische Studien*, 36, 1954, pp. 82–109
and 205–64.
16 This is the attempt by K. Esser, *Das Testament des Hl. Franziscus von Assisi.
Eine Untersuchung über seine Echtheit und Bedeutung*, Münster/W., 1949.
17 They are listed, with a short introduction, in O. Englebert, *Vie de saint
François d'Assise*, Paris, 1956[2], pp. 400–4.
18 I *Regula*, XXII.
19

all the following orders, the priests, deacons, subdeacons,
acolytes, exorcists, lectors, ushers and all the clergy, all the religious, both male and female, all the children and little children
of both genders, poor and indigent, kings and princes, workers
and farmers, serfs and masters, all the virgins, continent and
married, laity, men and women, all the little children, adolescents, young and old, healthy and sick, all the humble and the
great and all the people, families, tribes and languages, all the
nations and all the people everywhere on earth, who are and
will be . . .
(omnes sequentes ordines: sacerdotes, diaconos, subdiaconos,
acolythos, exorcistas, lectores, ostiarios et omnes clericos, uni-
versos religiosos et religiosas, omnes pueros et parvulos et par-
vulas, pauperes et egenos, reges et principes, laboratores et
agricolas, servos et dominos, omnes virgines et continentes et
maritatas, laicos, masculos et feminas, omnes infantes, adolescentes, iuvenes et senes, sanos et infirmos, omnes pusillos et
magnos et omnes populos, gentes, tribus et linguas, omnes
nationes et omnes homines ubicumque terrarum, qui sunt et
erunt . . .)

(I *Regula*, XXIII)

20 *Vita secunda*, 106, p. 193.
21 *Ibid.*, 200, p. 244.

22 'Almighty God most high, most sacred and supreme, Father holy and just, Lord King of heaven and earth' ('Omnipotens, altissime, sanctissime et summe Deus, Pater sancte et iuste, Domine Rex coeli et terrae.') (I *Regula*, XXIII).
23 *Salutatio Virginis Mariae*, I.
24 *Officium Passionis*, I, C, 12.
25 *Ibid.*
26 *Ibid.*
27 I *Regula*, IX, 6; *Regula Clarissarum*, II, 1; 'First Letter to the Faithful', 5.
28 Prayer 'Sancta Dei Genitrix Dulcis et Decora' (a work of dubious origin).
29 I *Regula*, XXI, 8–9.
30

> The agents of our Lord are the demons by whom he intends to punish excesses . . . and that is perhaps why he allows his agents to burst in on me, because my house does not look good enough to others in the court of the great.
>
> (Daemones sunt gastaldi Domini nostri, quos destinat ipse ad puniendos excessus . . . sed potest esse quod ideo gastaldos suos in me permisit irrumpere, quia non bonam speciem aliis praefert mansio mea in curia magnatorum.)
>
> (*Vita secunda*, 120, p. 201)

Saint Bonaventure, who takes up this passage again (*Legenda major*, VI, 10, p. 586), does not mention the *gastaldi*.
31 For example:

> all my brothers . . . as much the clergy as the laity
> (omnes fratres meos. . . tam clericos quam laicos)
> (I *Regula*, XVII)

> Forthwith many good and seemly men, clergy and laity, fleeing the world and the devil by the grace and the will of the Almighty followed him piously and courageously in their life and in their intention.
> (Statim namque quamplures boni et idonei viri, clerici et laici, fugientes mundum et diabolum viriliter elidentes gratia et voluntate Altissimi, vita et proposito eum devote secuti sunt.)
> (*Vita prima*, 56, p. 43)

32 For example:

> he wanted that the great unite with the small, the wise people with the simple, through a brotherly affection, and that those who were far away join with one another through the bond of love. See there, he says, all the religious who are in the Church

138

form a single general chapter! Because the learned and the ignorant are together.

(uniri volebat majores minoribus, germano affectu coniungi sapientes simplicibus, longinquos longinquis amoris glutino copulari . . . Ecce, ait, fiat omnium religiosorum qui in Ecclesia sunt unum capitulum generale! Quoniam igitur adsunt litterati et qui sine litteris sunt) (Acts 4:13).

(*Vita secunda*, 191, p. 240)

33 'Omnes fratres meos predicatores, oratores, laboratores' (I *Regula*, XVII). I do not believe that this sentence should be seen as presenting a new tripartite schema in which the *predicatores* would replace the *bellatores*, with preaching as a sort of verbal battle. The *oratores* usually come first, and it seems that this is a pair: 'oratores, laboratores' is immediately echoed by 'tam clericos quam laicos'.

34 Cf. Ch. Thouzellier, 'Ecclesia militans', in *Études d'histoire du droit canonique dédiées à Gabriel Le Bras*, Paris, 1965, vol. II, pp. 1407–23.

35 *Vita prima*, 53, p. 4. 'Brother Francis their servant and subject' ('Frater Franciscus eorum servus et subditus') (*Epistola omnibus fidelibus*).

36 *Ibid*.

37 *Ibid*., also in Julian of Speyer, *Vita*, 33, p. 351; Bonaventure, *Legenda major*, VI, 1, p. 582.

38 *Ibid*., Thomas of Celano adds, '*mercenarium* et inutilis', a probable reply to the doctrine of *utilitas* then in fashion among jurists and urban rulers. Francis was not the only one then to protest against this trend towards 'utilitarianism'.

39 'Alpigena et mercator' (Henri d'Avranches, *Legenda versificata*, VII, 116, p. 452). 'He preferred to call himself a mountain dweller and a mercenary/ Blaming himself for being an unarmed rustic' ('Sed magis alpigenam mercenariumque vocavit/Improperando sibi quod iners et rusticus esset') (*ibid*., XII, 8–9, p. 515).

40 I *Regula*, IX.

41 'And we were unlettered and obedient to all' ('Et eramus idiote et subditi omnibus') (*Testamentum*, 4). On poverty and the poor in the writings of Saint Francis, cf. Willibrord, *Le Message spirituel*, see 'Poverty', pp. 284–8; S. Clasen, 'Die Armut als Beruf: Franziskus von Assisi', in *Miscellanea Mediaevalia*, vol. III, Berlin, 1964, pp. 73–85.

42 I *Regula*, II.

43 In the story of the death of Saint Francis, Thomas of Celano writes: 'many of the brothers, whose father and leader he was, assembling near him' ('convenientibus itaque multis fratribus, quorum ipse pater et dux erat') (*Vita prima*, 110, p. 86).

44 'May each one love and nurture his brother as a mother loves and nurtures her son' ('Et quilibet diligat et nutriat fratrem suum, sicut mater diligit et nutrit filium suum') (I *Regula*, IX).

45

May those who want to live religiously in the hermitages be three or four brothers at the most. May two of them be the mothers and have two sons or at least one. May the ones behave like Martha and the others like Mary Magdalene. (Illi qui volunt religiose stare in heremis, sint tres fratres aut quatuor ad plus. Duo ex ipsis sint matres et habeant duos filios vel unum ad minus. Illi autem tenant vitam Marthe at alii duo vitam Marie Magdalene.)

(*De religiosa habitatione in eremo*)

46 'So I say you my son, like a mother' ('Ita diuco tibi, fili mi, et sicut mater') (*Epistola ad fratrem Leonem*).

47

And they will be the sons of the heavenly Father . . . whose works they do, and they are the spouses, the brothers, and the mothers of Our Lord Jesus Christ. We are his spouses, when our soul faithful to Jesus Christ unites with the Holy Spirit. We are his brothers, when we do the will of the Father, who is in heaven. . . . We are his mothers, when we bear him in our heart and body through love and pure and sincere consciousness, and we give birth to him through a holy operation that must shine as an example in the eyes of others. (Et erunt filii Patris celestis [Matt. 5:35] cuius opera faciunt, et sunt sponsi, fratres et matres Domini nostri Iesu Christi. Sponsi sumus, quando Spiritu Sancto coniungitur fidelis anima Iesu Christo. Fratres eius sumus, quando facimus voluntatem Patris eius, qui est in celo [Matt. 12:50]. Matres eius sumus, quando portamus eum in corde et corpore nostro per amorem et puram et sinceram conscientiam parturimus eum per sanctam operationem que lucere debet aliis in exemplum.)

(*Epistola ad fideles*, 9)

48 See above p. 137.

49 On this desocialisation of language, see J. Le Goff, 'Les paysans et le monde rural dans la littérature du haut Moyen Âge (Ve–VIe siècles)', in *L'agricoltura e il mondo rurale nell'alto medioevo. Settimane di Studio del Centro italiano di studi sull'alto medioevo* (Spoleto), XIII, 1966, pp. 723–41; also in Jacques Le Goff, *Pour un autre Moyen Âge*, Paris, 1977, pp. 131–44.

50 We have studied the formation and the significance of this pattern in a 'Note' presented to the colloquium on 'La formation des États européens, IXe–XIe siècles' (Warsaw, 1965) whose acts have appeared under the title *L'Europe aux IXe-XIe siècles. Aux origines des États nationaux*, Institut d'histoire de l'Académie polonaise des sciences, Warsaw, 1968; also in *Pour un autre Moyen Âge*, pp. 80–90.

51 'This saint . . . in beginning the three well-known orders' ('Iste sanctus . . . qui tres celebres ordines . . . inchoans') (Julian of Speyer, *Vita*, 15, p. 342).

52 'Therefore every order, each gender, and every age has in itself the proofs of the salutary doctrine' ('Omnis proinde ordo, omnis sexus, omnis aetas habet in ipso doctrinae salutaris evidentia documenta') (*Vita prima*, 94, p. 68).

53 Matt. 9:35; *Vita prima*, 62, p. 47.

54 Cf. the project described in note 4. At Arezzo, a prey to civil war, the biographers note that the saint was received 'in the village outside the city' ('in burgo extra civitatem') (*Vita secunda*, 108) and 'in the suburbs' ('in suburbio') (Bonaventure, *Legenda major*, VI, 9).

55 On a type of neighbouring habitat, cf. G. Duby, 'Recherches récentes sur la vie rurale en Provence au XIVe siècle', *Provence historique*, 1965, pp. 97–111.

56 *Vita prima*, 62, p. 47.

57 *Ibid.*, 31, p. 25.

58 Cf. G. H. Williams, *The Layman in Christian History*, London, 1963; 'I laici nella società religiosa dei secoli XI–XII' (Colloquium of Passo della Mendola, 1965); A. Frugoni, 'Considerazioni sull' "ordo laicorum" nella reforma gregoriana' (XIe Congrès international des sciences historiques, Stockholm, 1960, *Résumés des communications*, pp. 119–20, *Actes du Congrès*, p. 136); A. Vauchez, *Les Laïcs au Moyen Âge. Pratiques et expériences religieuses*, Paris, 1987.

59 'When he entered a city, the clergy rejoiced, the bells rang out, the men exulted, the women were jubilant, the children clapped their hands' ('Ingrediente ipso aliquam civitatem, laetabatur clerus, pulsabantur campanae, exsultabant viri, congaudebant feminae, applaudebant pueri') (*Vita prima*, 62, p. 47; cf. Julian of Speyer, *Vita*, 46, p. 357, and *Legenda monacensis*, 42, p. 706); 'The men ran, the women rushed forward, the clergy made haste, the religious hurried . . . people of all ages and all sexes hastened' ('Currebant viri, currebant et feminae, festinabant clerici, accelerabant religiosi. . . omnis aetas omnisque sexus properabat').

60 'And many of the people, nobles and commoners, clergy and laity, began to come to Saint Francis' ('Coeperunt multi de populo, nobiles et ignobiles, clerici et laici . . . ad sanctum Franciscum accedere') (*Vita prima*).

61 'And may he not value one thousand powerful people more than a single poor man. Nor a thousand scholars more than a single simple man' ('Verum non uno plus paupere mille potentes/Extimet, aut uno plus simplice mille peritos') (*Legenda versificata*, IX, 176–7, p. 468).

62 'Any of the faithful, rich, poor, noble, common, worthless, brilliant, prudent, simple, cleric, famous, lay, among the Christian people' ('Aliquis, quicumque ac qualiscumque fidelis, dives, pauper, nobilis, ignobilis, vilis, arus, prudens, simplex, clericus, idiota, laicus in populo christiano') (*Vita prima*, 31, p. 25). This list can be compared to the one in which Henri d'Avranches surveys all the social categories whose members had entered the Order of the Minors:

May no condition, fortune, or age,
Be refused: may everyone be admitted
Without exception, the good and the evil, the high and the low,
The peasant and the knight, the common and the noble,
The clergy and the laity, the gross and the refined, the poor
And the rich, the serf and the freeman, the healthy and the sick;
Francis received them all in his pious affection.

non conditio, fortuna vel aetas,
(Ulla recusatur: veniens admittitur omnis
Et sine delectu, bonus et malus, altus et imus,
Rusticus et miles, ignobilis et generosus,
Clericus et laicus, rudis et discretus, egenus
Et dives, servus et liber, sanus et aeger;
Affectuque pio Franciscus suscipit omnes.)
(*Legenda versificata*, VI, 34–40, pp. 443–4)

63 'If invited by lords' ('Si quando invitatus a dominis') (*Vita secunda*, 72, p. 174).

64 'If invited by important people' ('Si quando invitatus a magnis personis') (Bonaventure, *Legenda major*, VII, 7, p. 589).

65 *Vita prima*, 51, p. 40.

66 'Received at any time among the great' ('Inter magnates ut quandocumque receptus') (*Legenda versificata*, VII, 113, p. 452).

67 'A knight of this same city received him as a guest' ('Miles quidam eiusdem civitatis eum suscepit hospitio') (*Vita prima*, 65, p. 49).

68 'Strive to be so good that you will be celebrated by all, for many have faith in you' ('Stude, ait rusticus, adeo bonus esse, ut ab omnibus diceris, quia multi confidunt de te') (*Vita secunda*, 142, p. 212).

69 *Ibid.*, 46, p. 159.

70 *Vita prima*, 44, p. 35.

71 *Ibid.*, 37, p. 30.

72 *Ibid.*, 16, p. 15.

73 'Praeco sum magni Regis.' 'Iace, rustice praeco Dei.'

74 *Vita secunda*, 4, p. 132.

75
Because he was very rich, not avaricious but generous, not an hoarder of money but a great spender, a prudent merchant but a very big wastrel.
(Quia praedives erat, non avarus sed prodigus, non accumulator pecuniae sed substantiae dissipator, cautus *negotiator sed vanissimus dispensator.*)
(*Vita prima*, 2, p. 7)

76 'He was not used to seeing such objects in his house, but rather piles of cloth for sale' ('Non enim consueverat talia in domo sua videre sed potius pannorum cumulos ad vendendum') (*Vita prima*, 5, pp. 8–9).

77 *Vita secunda*, 31; Bonaventure, *Legenda major*, XI, 8, p. 608.

78 'He became a merchant of the Gospels' ('Evangelicus negotiator efficitur') (Julian of Speyer, *Vita*, I, 3, p. 337).

79 *Vita prima*, 8, p. ii. The expression comes from St Paul: 2 Tim. 1:3. Thomas of Celano, using this traditional image, nevertheless underscores Saint Francis's originality by writing: '*novus* Christi miles'. Cf. H. Felder, *Der Christusritter aus Assisi*, Zurich and Altstetten, 1941.

80 *Vita prima*, 93, p. 71.

81 *Ibid.*, 103, p. 80.

82 'Thus the mirror of the great and chief of the Minors,/For the minor on earth becomes major in heaven' ('Sic igitur speculum majorum, duxque Minorum,/Quo minor in terris est major in ethere') (*Legenda versificata*, XIV, 82–3, p. 488). But the source may be the story already cited of the death of Francis in Thomas of Celano: 'ipse pater et dux erat' (*Vita prima*, 110, p. 86). It is a borrowing from the New Testament: 'ipse dux erat' (Acts 14:11).

83 'Brothers who militate personally under the leadership of such a great chief' ('Fratres, sub tanto duce personaliter militantes') (23, p. 346).

84 'And himself like the good chief of the army of Christ' ('Et ipse tanquam bonus dux exercitus Christi') (*Legenda major*, V, 10, p. 577; XIII, 10, p. 620).

85 Inspired by Ps. 73:12, 'You have ground the head of the dragon' ('Tu confregisti capita draconis'), the hymn has a very military and chivalrous language and spirit (p. 401). On the *dux* theme, Thomas of Capua, cardinal of Sainte-Sabine, had composed in the honour of Francis a hymn for vespers that Julian of Speyer would incorporate in his *Officium rhythmicum* (p. 386).

86 'Omnes theologos et qui ministrant sanctissima verba divina debemus honorare et venerari' (*Testamentum*, 3), cited by Thomas of Celano (*Vita secunda*, 163, p. 224), who compares it to the letter to Anthony of Padua.

87

> And for him the principal cause of the reverence of the doctors, was that, as auxiliaries of Christ, they fulfilled their office with Christ.
> (Et haec penes eum causa potissima venerandi doctores, quod Christi adiutores unum cum Christo exsequerentur officium.)
>
> (*Vita secunda*, 172, p. 230)

> He especially honoured the priests and revered the theologians with an admirable affection.
> (Honorabat praecipue sacerdotes et divinae legis doctores miro venerabatur affectu.)
>
> (*Legenda chori*, 6, p. 121)

88 The four Franciscan masters would develop this with much lucidity in their comments on the Rule, in 1241–42, (*Expositio Quatuor Magistrorum super Regulam Fratrum Minorum*, ed. L. Oliger, Rome, 1950).

89

> He saw many of them turning to the directing power of the masters, whose temerity he detested, and he exhorted them to turn away from this plague towards his example.
> (Videbat enim multos ad magisterii regimina convolare, quorum temeritatem detestans, ab huiusmodi peste sui exemplo revocare studebat eos.)
>
> (*Vita prima*, 104, p. 80)

The biographers complaisantly expanded on the reception of the *litterati* in the Order by Saint Francis, while underscoring the state of mind that the saint expected:

> He said that a great cleric should renounce even knowledge when he entered the Order, so that, freed of this possession, he could give himself naked in the arms of the Crucifix.
> (Dixit aliquando magnum clericum etiam scientiae quodammodo resignare debere, cum veniret ad Ordinem, sub tali expropriatus possessione, nudum se offeret brachiis Crucifix.)
>
> (*Vita secunda*, 194, p. 241)

> He who wishes to attain this summit must renounce not only worldly wisdom, but also book learning, so that, freed of this possession, he can enter into the power of the Lord and offer himself naked in the arms of the Crucifix.
> (Ad huius, inquit culmen qui cupit attingere, non solum mundanae prudentiae, verum etiam litterarum peritiae renuntiare quodammodo debet, ut, tali expropriatus possessione, introeat in potentiam Domini et nudum se offerat brachiis Crucifixi.)
>
> (Bonaventure, *Legenda major*, VII, 2, p. 587)

Cf. the whole chapter 'De sancta simplicitate', in *Vita secunda*, 189–95, pp. 238–42. When Thomas of Celano speaks of the particular devotion for Saint Francis in France, among Louis IX, Blanche of Castile and the great (*magnates*), he adds:

> Even the wise and the very learned people of the earth, of whom Paris produces more than anywhere else, humbly and very piously admire and honour Francis, an illiterate man and a friend of true simplicity and total sincerity.
> (Etiam sapientes orbis et litteratissimi viri, quorum copiam super omnem terram Parisius maximam ex more producit, Franciscum

virum idiotam et verae simplicitatis totiusque sinceritatis amicum, humiliter et devotissime venerantur, admirantur et colunt.)

(*Vita prima*, 120, p. 95)

90

He said that the Son of God had descended from the greatness of the Father to our contemptible lowness, so that the Lord and Master could teach by word and by example. That is why he strove, as a disciple of Christ, to make himself small in his own eyes and in those of others, remembering that the Very High Master had said: that which is high for people is an abomination for God.

(Dicebat, propter hoc Filium Dei de altitudine sinus paterni ad nostra despicabilia descendisse, ut tam exemplo quam verbo Dominus et Magister humilitatem doceret. Propter quod studebat tanquam Christi discipulus in oculis suis et aliorum vilescere a summo dictum esse Magistro commemorans: Quod altum est apud homines, abominatio est apud Deum) (Luke 16:15).

(Bonaventure, *Legenda major*, VI, 1, p. 582)

This thematic unity is very representative of the ability of Saint Bonaventure, a peacemaking arbiter of the Order's diverse tendencies.

91 *Vita secunda*, 82–4, pp. 180–1.

92 II *Regula*, VI. This is another borrowing from Paul (2 Cor. 8:2).

93 'True lover of poverty, sometimes like a mother, sometimes like a wife, sometimes like a mistress' ('Verus paupertatis amator, quam modo matrem, modo sponsam, modo dominam') (*Legenda major*, VI, 2, p. 586).

94 *Vita secunda*, 5, p. 133; Bonaventure, *Legenda major*, I, 3, p. 561; *Legenda minor*, I, 3, p. 656.

95 Cf. W. Ullmann, *The Individual and Society in the Middle Ages*, Baltimore, 1966, pp. 10 ff.; C. Morris, *The Discovery of the Individual (1050–1200)*, New York, 1972.

96 Ullmann, *The Individual and Society*, pp. 12–13.

97 In Rockinger, *Briefsteller und Formelbücher*, Munich, 1863, p. 186, cited by Ullmann, *The Individual and Society*, p. 18, n. 38.

98 Rockinger, *Briefsteller*, pp. 361 ff., 727, cited by Ullmann, *The Individual and Society*, p. 17, n. 36.

99 On the *septem rectores super capitibus artium* mentioned in Florence in 1193, cf. A. Doren, *Le arti fiorentine*, Ital. trans., Florence, 1940, I, p. 6. On the *custodes* of Toulouse, cf. M. A. Mulholland, *Early Gild Records of Toulouse*, New York, 1941; *idem*, 'Statutes on Clothmaking. Toulouse, 1227', in *Essays in Medieval Life and Thought Presented in Honor of Austin Patterson Evans*, New York, 1955, pp. 167 ff.; A. Gouron, *La Réglementation des métiers en Languedoc au Moyen Âge*, Geneva and Paris, 1958, pp. 204–5.

100 On *minister* = apprentice, see C. Klapisch-Zuber, *Le Marbre de Carrare*, Paris, 1969.

101 It is impossible to recall here all the works concerning the relationships of Franciscanism with the society of its time. The question has been well defined by L. Salvatorelli, 'Movimento francescano e gioachimismo. La storiografia francescana contemporanea', X *Congresso internazionale di scienze storiche, Relazioni*, III (*Storia del Medioevo*), Rome, 1955, pp. 403– 48. An interesting sketch by Fr Willibrord and C. Van Dijk is *Signification sociale du franciscanisme naissant*, Paris, 1965. Cf., despite the absence of a concrete sociological dimension, K. Esser, *Anfänge und ursprungliche Zersetzungen des Ordens der Minderbrüder*, Leyden, 1966.

102 For an understanding of the wider context in which Franciscan thought is situated, see R. Hund Eberstadt, *Magisterium et Fraternitas*, Leipzig, 1897.

103 Cf. L. Mumford, *The City in History: its Origins, its Transformations, and its Prospects*, New York, 1961, pp. 312 ff.

104

So that the bond of love between the brothers should be greater, he wanted his whole Order to be joined in uniformity, the great with the minors, the literate with the illiterate, united by the same behaviour and way of living like in the house of a single family.

(Ut major esset inter fratres caritatis societas, voluit totum Ordinem suum esse uniformitate concordem ubi majores minoribus, litterati illiteratis simili habitu et vitae observantia unirentur . . . ut quasi unius domu familia.)

(*Vita secunda*, 191, p. 240)

105

Because of the virtue of humility, he did not want the leaders of the Order to be referred to in the Rule as dignities, abbots, superintendents or priors, but instead as ministers and custodians, so that it would be clear that they were the servants rather than the masters of the brothers.

(Propter humiliatis quoque virtutem noluit rectores Ordinis nominibus dignitatum in Regula appellare abbates, praepositos vel priores, sed ministros et custodes, ut per hoc intelligant, se fratrum suorum potius servitores esse quam dominos.)

(*Legenda monacencis*, p. 709)

106

As the cardinal of Ostia had asked him . . . if he would like his brothers to be promoted to the ecclesial dignities, he replied: Lord, I have wanted that my brothers be known as Minors so that they do not dream of being great. If you want their actions to be fruitful in the Church, keep them in the state of their vocation and do not allow them to rise to ecclesial prelacies. (Cum autem requiret ab eo dominus Ostiensis . . . utrum sibi placeret quod fratres sui promoverentur ad ecclesiasticas dignitates, respondit: Domine, Minores ideo vocati sunt fratres mei ut majores fieri non presumant. Si vultis ut fructum faciant in Ecclesia Dei tenete illos et conservate in statu vocationis eorum, et ad praelationes ecclesiasticas nullatenus ascendere permittatis.)

(*Legenda major*, VI, 5, p. 584)

Cf. *Vita secunda*,148, p. 216.

107 The notion of peace is essential in the thought and the apostolate of Saint Francis. 'When they enter into a house, let them first say: Peace on this house' ('In quacumque domum intraverint, primum dicant: Pax huic domui') (II *Regula*, III). 'The Lord has revealed this salutation to me so that we say: may the Lord give you peace' ('Salutationem mihi Dominus revelavit, ut diceremus: Dominus det tibi pacem') (*Testamentum*, 6). This recalls the peacemaker Saint Louis, who was greatly influenced by Franciscanism. On the early Franciscans and politics, see A. Vauchez, 'Une campagne de pacification en Lombardie autour de 1233. L'action politique des ordres mendiants d'après la réforme des statuts communaux et les accords de paix', *Mélanges d'archéologie et d'histoire*, 78, 1966, pp. 503–49.

108 'The Saint said to him: I do not want to be a thief; we will be called thieves if we do not give more to the destitute' ('Cui sanctus: Ego fur esse nolo; pro furto nobis imputaretur, si non daremus magis egenti'). Cf. II *Regula*, IX: 'Alms-giving is the heritage and the justice that is owed to the poor' ('Elemosina est hereditas et institia, que debetur pauperibus').

109
> If a minister prescribes a brother something against our way of life or against our soul, the brother is not held to obey him, because there is no disobedience where there is crime or sin.
> (Si quis autem ministrorum alicui fratrum aliquid contra vitam nostram vel contra animam suam preciperet, frater non teneatur ei obedire, quia illa obedientia non est, in qua delictum vel peccatum committitur.)

(I *Regula*, V)

110 Cf. K. Esser, 'Die Handarbeit in der Frühgeschichte des Minderbrüderordens', *Franziskanische Studien*, 40, 1958.

111 Cf. L. Hardick, 'Pecunia et denarii. Untersuchung zum Geldverbot in den Regeln der Minderbrüder', *Franziscanische Studien*, 40, 1958. On class struggle in thirteenth-century Italy, see the classic work of G. Salvemini, *Magnati e popolani a Firenze*, Florence, 1899, and G. Fasoli, 'La legislazione antimagnatizia nei comuni dell'alta e media Italia', *Rivista di storia del diritto*

italiano, and, especially, from the perspective here retained, G. Fasoli, 'Gouvernants et gouvernés dans les communes italiennes du XIe au XIIIe siècle', *Recueils de la Société Jean Bodin*, XXV, 1965, pp. 47–86.

112 On poverty in the Middle Ages, the most important recent research is by M. Mollat and his students. Two provisional outlines have been given: M. Mollat, 'Pauvres et pauvreté à la fin du XIIe siècle', *Revue d'ascétique et de mystique*, 1965, pp. 305–23; idem, 'La notion de pauvreté au Moyen Âge: position du problème', *Revue d'histoire de l'Église de France*, 1967 (see this whole issue and notably G. Duby, 'Les pauvres des campagnes dans l'Occident médiéval jusqu'au XIIIe siècle'). More recently, see M. Mollat, *Les Pauvres au Moyen Âge. Étude sociale*, Paris, 1978. Poverty in the twelfth century was the subject of the colloquium of the Academia Tudertina, Todi, 1967. Let us recall, framing our period, E. Werner, *Pauperes Christi, Studien zu Sozial-Religiösen Bewegungen im Zeitalter des Reformpapsttums*, Leipzig, 1956; F. Graus, 'Au bas Moyen Âge: pauvres des villes et pauvres des campagnes', *Annales, E.S.C.*, 1961, pp. 1053–65; especially important for our problematics, K. Bosl, 'Potens und Pauper', *Festschrift für O. Brunner*, Göttingen, pp. 60–87, also in *Frühformen der Gesellschaft im mittelalterlichen Europa*, Munich, 1964.

113 For an example of the development of a national consciousness (without political outcome) placed in a study of global history, see P. Vilar, *La Catalogne dans l'Espagne moderne*, Paris, 1963. On the vicissitudes of poverty in the post-medieval Mediterranean world, see F. Braudel, *La Méditerranée et le monde méditerranéen à l'époque de Philippe II*, 2nd edn, Paris, 1966, II, pp. 75 ff., and E. J. Hobsbawm, *Primitive Rebels: Studies in Archaic Forms of Social Movement in the 19th and 20th Centuries*, Manchester, 1959.

114 On Francis of Assisi and the society of his time, two interesting essays are: S. Clasen, 'Franziscus von Assisi und die soziale Frage', *Wissenschaft und Weisheit*, 15, 1952, pp. 109–21; H. Roggen, 'Die Lebensform des heiligen Franziskus von Assisi in ihren Verhältnis zur feudalen und bürgerlichen Gesellschaft Italiens', *Franziskanische Studien*, XLVI, 1964, pp. 1–57 and 287–321.

4 Franciscanism and cultural models of the thirteenth century

1 A. Benvenuti Papi, 'L'impianto mendicante in Firenze, un problema apero', in *Les Ordres Mendiants et la ville en Italie centrale (v. 1220–v.1350)*, (Roundtable discussion at the École française de Rome), Rome, 1977, pp. 595–608.

2 A. I. Galletti, 'Insediamento degli ordini mendicanti nella città di Perugia. Prime considerazioni e appunti di ricerca', *ibid.*, pp. 587–94.

3 L. Gatto, 'Il sentimento cittadino nella "Cronica" di Salimbene', in *La coscienza cittadina nei comuni italiani del Duecento*, Todi, 1972, pp. 365–94. Cf. C. Violante, 'Motivi e carattere della Cronica di Salimbene', *Annali della Scuola normale superiore di Pisa*, s. II, 22, 1953.

4 L. Pellegrini, 'L'ordine francescano e la società cittadina in epoca bona-
venturiana. Un'analisi del "Determinationes quaestionum super Regulam
Fratrum Minorum"', *Laurentianum*, 15, 1974, pp. 175–7. Cf. J. Le Goff,
'Ordres mendiants et urbanisation dans la France médiévale', *Annales*.
E.S.C., 1970, pp. 928–31.

5 'The brothers known as Minors [. . .] living in the towns and cities' ('Fratres
qui dicuntur Minores . . . habitantes in urbibus et civitatibus') (*Historia
Anglorum*, in *Monumenta Germaniae Historica, Scriptorum*, vol. XXVIII,
397, ad annum 1207).

6 For example, Francis preaching in 1222 in the square in front of the public
palace, in Bologna, where 'almost the whole city was assembled' (Thomas
of Spalato, *Historia Salonitarum*, in L. Lemmens, *Testimonia minora saeculi
XIII de S. Francisco Assisiensi*, Quaracchi, 1926, p. 10).

7
> In Limoges, as he had called the people to a sermon, and the
> crowd was so great that all the churches were too small, he con-
> voked the people to a spacious place that had formerly been the
> palace of the pagans and that was known as the pit of Arenis.
> ('Cum semel Lemovicus populum ad praedicationem convo-
> casset, et tanta esset multitudo populi quod angusta reputaretur
> quaelibet ecclesia . . . ad quemdam locum spatiosum, ubi olim
> fuerant palatia paganorum, qui locus dicitur Fovea de Arenis,
> populum convocavit.)
>
> (*AA.SS.*, *Junii*, II, 727, cited by A. Lecoy de La Marche,
> *La Chaire française au Moyen Âge, spécialement au XIIIe siècle*,
> Paris, 1886, p. 141)

8 Le Goff, 'Ordres mendiants et urbanisations', p. 932. Cf. E. Guidoni, 'Città
e ordini mendicanti', in *La città dal medioevo al rinascimento*, Bari, 1981,
pp. 123–58.

9 P. Michaud-Quantin, *Universitas. Expressions du mouvement communautaire
dans le Moyen Âge latin*, Paris, 1970, especially pp. 78–9.

10 The text of the *Regula non bullata* is, 'And in whatever house they enter, let
them say first: Peace on this house' ('Et in quamcumque domum intraverint, dicant primum: Pax huic domui') (XIV). Cf. C. Esser (ed.), *Opuscula Sancti Patris Francisci Assisiensis*, Grottaferrata, 1978, Indices, see
'domus', p. 370. The sentence is repeated in the *Regula bullata*.

11 *Legenda trium sociorum*, 60.

12 *Ibid.*, 37.

13 Cf. *ibid.*, 60, which could be translated as, 'When they could not be
received by priests, they preferred to go to the homes of pious and God-
fearing men.'

14 *Vita secunda*, 58.

15 B. Smalley, 'Ecclesiastical Attitudes to Novelty c. 1100–c. 1250', in
D. Baker (ed.), *Church, Society and Politics*, Oxford, 1975, pp. 113–31.

16 *Analecta franciscana*, vol. 10, 1926–41, p. 402.

NOTES

17 Lemmens, *Testimonia minora*, p. 17.

18 *Legend of Perugia* (henceforth cited as *Leg. Per.*), 114. Note the word *pazzo* (*pazzus*) from the vernacular language.

19 F. De Beer, *La Conversion de saint François selon Thomas de Celano*, Paris, 1963.

20 Besides the classic essay by Luigi Salvatorelli, 'Movimento francescano e gioachimismo. La storiografia francescana contemporanea', in *X Congresso Internazionale di scienze storiche, Relazioni*, III (*Storia del Medioevo*), Florence, 1955, pp. 403–48, from an abundant literature, see among others, F. Russo, 'S. Francesco ed i Francescani nella letteratura profetica gioachimita', in *Miscellanea francescana*, 46, 1946, pp. 232–42.

21 *Vita secunda*, p. 220.

22 Cf. Frances Yates, *The Art of Memory*, London, 1966.

23 De Beer, *La Conversion*, pp. 222–4.

24 C. Esser, *Opuscula*, p. 324: 'in sign of the memory of my benediction and of my testament' ('in signum memoriae meae benedictionis et mei testamenti').

25 'L'*assidua devotio* è la "memoria di Dio" presente in maniera stabile e continua "*ante oculos cordis*"' (Z. Zafarana, 'Pietà e devozione in San Bonaventura', in *San Bonaventura francescano* (Convegni del Centro di studi sulla spiritualità medievale, XIV), Todi, 1975, p. 134).

26 J. T. Noonan Jr., *The Scholastic Analysis of Usury*, Cambridge (Mass.), 1957, p. 60.

27 See, among others, J. Le Goff, 'Temps de l'Église et temps du marchand', *Annales. E.S.C.*, 15, 1960, pp. 417–33, also in J. Le Goff, *Pour un autre Moyen Âge: temps, travail, culture en occident*, Paris, 1977, pp. 46–65; J. Le Goff, 'The Usurer and Purgatory', in *The Dawn of Modern Banking*, New Haven (Conn.), Yale University Press, 1979, pp. 25–52; J. Le Goff, *La Bourse et la Vie. Économie et religion au Moyen Âge*, Paris, 1986. See especially L. K. Little, *Religious Poverty and the Profit Economy in Medieval Europe*, London, 1978.

28 Noonan, *The Scholastic Analysis*, p. 63. On the attitudes of Saint Francis to money, see, besides the passages cited of the two Rules: *Vita prima*, 9, 12: 'may he worry no more about money than about dust' ('de pecunia velut de pulivere curat'); *Vita secunda*, 65, 66–68; *Legenda trium sociorum*, 35; *Legenda major*, 7, 5; *Speculum perfectionis*, 14. On Judas, symbol of the diabolical nature of money for the Franciscans, see M. D. Lambert, *Franciscan Poverty*, London, 1961, 'Judas'.

29 See J. Le Goff, 'Métiers licites et métiers illicites dans l'Occident médiéval', *Études historiques, Annales de l'École des hautes études de Gand*, V, 1963, pp. 41–57, also in Le Goff, *Pour un autre Moyen Âge*, pp. 91–107.

30 *Vita Beati Fratris Egidii*, 5, in *Scripta Leonis, Rufini et Angeli sociorum S. Francisci*, ed. R. B. Brooke, Oxford, 1970, pp. 324–6.

31 *De adventu fratrum minorum in Angliam. The Chronicle of Thomas of Eccleston*, ed. A. G. Little, Manchester, 1951, pp. 5–6: 'who worked at

the beginning in a mechanical trade, according to the decree of the rule' ('qui laboravit in principio in opere mechanico, secundum decretum regulae').

32 See W. Kölmel, 'Labor und paupertas bei Bonaventura', in *San Bonaventura maestro di vita francescana e di sapienza cristiana* (Atti del Congresso internazionale per il VII centenario, di san Bonaventura da Bagnoregio), ed. A. Pompei, vol. II, Rome, 1976, pp. 569–82.

33 Cf. M. M. Dufeil, *Guillaume de Saint-Amour et la polémique universitaire parisienne, 1250–1259*, Paris, 1972, see 'travail intellectuel', 'travail manuel'.

34 Fr. Esser's edition of the *Opuscula* of Saint Francis does not retain the original addresses in its titles: letter to *all* the faithful, letter to *all* the clerics. These titles do not exist, of course, in the medieval manuscripts. However, the first lines of the writings of Saint Francis: 'all of them, male and female' ('omnes autem illi et illae'), 'to all the Christian religious, clergy and laity, men and women, to all who live in the entire world' ('universis christianis religiosis, clericis et laicis, masculis et feminis omnibus qui habitant in universo mundo'), 'let us, all the clerics, pay attention' ('attendamus, omnes clerici'), 'to all the powerful and all the consuls, judges and governors everywhere on earth and to all the others' ('universis potestatibus et consulibus, indicibus atque rectoribus ubique terrarum et omnibus aliis'), justify the traditional titles.

35 This analysis is outlined above in Chapter 3, pp. 63–96.

36 See the translation of this passage in Chapter 3 above, p. 137 n. 19.

37 G. de Lagarde, *La Naissance de l'esprit laïque au déclin du Moyen Âge*, 6 vols, new edn, Paris, 1956–63. On the place of the laity in thirteenth-century spirituality, see J. Leclerc, F. Vandenbroucke and L. Bouyer, *La Spiritualité du Moyen Âge*, Paris, 1961: 'Laïcs et clercs au XIIIe siècle', pp. 414–47.

38 J. Mundy, *Europe in the High Middle Ages 1150–1309*, London, 1973, pp. 186–7.

39 *De adventu fratrum minorum in Angliam*, 21.

40 R. Manselli, 'La clericalizzazione dei Minori e san Bonaventura', in *San Bonaventura*, pp. 181–208.

41 In F. De Beer, *La Conversion*, see 'Femme'. And also see J. Dalarun, *François d'Assise: un passage. Femme et féminité dans les écrits et légendes franciscaines*, Arles, 1997.

42 Latin text by R. B. C. Huygens, *Lettres de Jacques de Vitry*, Leyden, 1960, pp. 75–6.

43 G. Miccoli, 'La storia religiosa', in *Storia d'Italia, 2/1: Dalla caduta dell'impero romano al secolo XVIII*, Turin, 1974, pp. 825–31. On 'the complex discourse' of the Franciscans in preaching to women in the thirteenth century, see C. Casagrande, *Prediche alle donne del secolo XIII*, Milan, 1978, pp. xvii–xix, and the extracts from Gilbert de Tournai.

44 See G. Duby, *Le Chevalier, la Femme et le Prêtre. Le mariage dans la France féodale*, Paris, 1981.

45 Some versions give *conversos* and *parvulos*, others *pueros parvulos*, which seem, in both cases, to refer to children and to monastic oblates. On the increasing attention to children in the thirteenth century, see M. Rouche, *Histoire générale de l'enseignement et de l'éducation en France, I: Des origines à la Renaissance*, Paris, 1981, pp. 408–13.

46 See notably *Vita prima*, 84–7. The episode took place at Christmas 1223. Saint Francis had a special devotion for the feast of Christmas, when the *humility* of Jesus was manifested in the Incarnation.

47 In C. Esser, *Opuscula*, see 'Caritas'.

48 G. G. Meersseman, *Dossier de l'ordre de la Pénitence au XIIIe siècle*, Fribourg, 1961, p. 11, and Miccoli, 'La storia religiosa', p. 797.

49 Miccoli, 'La storia religiosa', p. 737.

50 See Chapter 3 above, pp. 90–2.

51 Marie-Claire Gasnault has indicated to me that Jacques de Vitry (bishop and, at the end of his life, cardinal!), in his *Sermones ad status*, is especially severe with the *praelati*, to whom he devotes eight sermons, while no other *status* got more than three.

52 Michaud-Quantin, *Universitas*, p. 105.

53 *Ibid.*, pp. 315–19, on 'consortium'.

54 *Ibid.*, pp. 179–92, on 'fraternitas' and 'confraternitas'; pp. 197–200, on 'caritas'.

55 See Chapter 3 above, pp. 73–6.

56 T. Desbonnets and D. Vorreux, *Saint François d'Assise. Documents, écrits et premières biographies*, Paris, 1981², see 'Savants', p. 1548.

57 Cf. *Le scuole degli Ordini Mendicanti*, Todi, 1978 (Convegni del Centro di studi sulla spiritualità medievale, 17).

58 *De adventu fratrum minorum in Angliam*, 74.

59 Cf. P. Gratien de Paris, *Histoire de la fondation et de l'évolution de l'ordre des frères Mineurs au XIIIe siècle*, Paris and Gembloux, 1928, pp. 269–75. On knowledge and poverty, see D. Berg, *Armut und Wissenschaft. Beitrage zur Geschichte des Studienwesens der Bettelorden im 13. Jahrhundert*, Düsseldorf, 1977.

60 On the basis of the Mendicants' right to preach, see M. Peuchmaurd, 'Mission canonique et prédication', *Recherches de théologie ancienne et mediévale*, 19, 1962, pp. 122–44 and 251–76, and P.-M. Gy, 'Le statut ecclésiologique de l'apostolat des Prêcheurs et des Mineurs avant la querelle des Mendiants', *Revue des sciences philosophiques et théologiques*, 59, 1975, pp. 79–88.

61 Cf. A. Lecoy de La Marche, *La Chaire française*, pp. 209–15.

62 J. Le Goff and J.-Cl. Schmitt, 'Au XIIIe siècle, une parole nouvelle', in J. Delumeau (ed.), *Histoire vécue du peuple chrétien*, I, Toulouse, 1979, pp. 257–80.

63 Lemmens, *Testimonia minora*, p. 10; Desbonnets and Vorreux, *Saint François*, p. 1435.

64 *Legenda trium sociorum*, XIII, 54, ed. Th. Desbonnets, in *Archivum franciscanum historicum*, 67, 1974, p. 129.

65 See, for example, *La Tabula Exemplorum secundum ordinem alphabeti*, a work by a Franciscan in France at the end of the thirteenth century, ed. J. Th. Welter, reprint, Geneva, 1973. Cf. Cl. Bremond, J. Le Goff and J.-Cl. Schmitt, *L'Exemplum*, Fascicule 40 de la Typologie des Sources du Moyen Âge occidental, Turnhout, 1982.

66 D. Bigalli, 'Giudizio escatologico e tecnica di missione nei pensatori francescani: Ruggero Bacone', in *Espansione del francescanesimo tra Occidente e Oriente nel secolo XIII* (Atti del VI Convegno internazionale, Assisi, 1978), Assisi, 1979, p. 186. On the attitudes towards the crusade in the thirteenth century, see F. Cardini, 'La crociata nel Duecento, l'"avatara di un ideale"', *Archivio storico italiano*, 135, 1977, pp. 101–39.

67 R. Manselli, 'De la "persuasio" a la "coercitio"', in *Le Credo, la Morale et l'Inquisition* (Cahiers de Fanjeaux, 6) Toulouse, 1971, pp. 175–98. On the Minors and the Inquisition in Italy in the thirteenth century, M. D'Alatri, *L'inquisizione francescana nell' Italia centrale nel sec. XIII*, Rome, 1954, and L. Paolini, 'Gli ordini mendicanti e l'Inquisizione: il "comportamento" degli eretici e il giudizio sui frati', in *Les Ordres mendiants et la ville en Italie centrale*, pp. 695–709.

68 Cf. C. Delcorno, 'Predicazione volgare e volgarizzamenti', in *Les Ordres mendiants et la ville*, pp. 679–89.

69 F. Demarchi, '*Una prospettiva sociologica dell'evoluzione della liturgia medioevale in teatro religioso*', in *Dimensioni drammatiche della liturgia medioevale* (Atti del I Convegno di Studio del Centro di Studi sul teatro medioevale e rinascimentale, Viterbo, 1976), Rome, 1977, p. 303.

It would be worthwhile to identify and study Franciscan theatrical body language, as mentioned by Thomas of Celano in the case of Saint Francis, who organised actual scenarios (preaching in the square of Assisi, then entering the cathedral crypt and returning without a habit, a cord around his neck; preaching at Greccio, where his gestures were noted; preaching before Honorius III where Francis 'danced somehow, not like an acrobat, but like a man burnt by God's love'). Or sometimes dramatic turns were used, as during the sermon of Brother Gerardo on the Piazza del Comune in Parma: Salimbene says that the preacher stopped suddenly to hide his face in his hood.

70 *De adventu*, 91–2.

71 A. Murray, *Reason and Society in the Middle Ages*, Oxford, 1978, p. 182.

72 G. Duby, 'La vulgarisation des modèles culturels dans la société féodale', in *Niveaux de culture et groupes sociaux*, Paris and The Hague, 1967, also in *Hommes et structures au Moyen Âge*, Paris and The Hague, 1973, pp. 299–309.

73 Desbonnets and Vorreux, *Saint François d'Assise. Documents rassemblés et présentés*, see 'Courtoisie', p. 1530.

74 Miccoli, 'La storia religiosa', pp. 735–6. But see also F. Cardini, 'San Francesco e il sogno delle armi', *Studi francescani*, 77, 1980, pp. 15–28.
75 Miccoli, 'La storia religiosa', p. 736.
76 Ed. F. Ageno, Florence, 1953, p. 233.
77 Luigi Salvatorelli, 'Movimento francescano e gioachimismo', p. 425, cited by R. Morghen, *Civiltà medioevale al tramonto*, V: *San Francesco e la tradizione francescana nella civiltà dell'Europa cristiana*, Bari, 1971, p. 66, Cf. R. Morghen, 'Francescanismo e Rinascimento', in *Iacopone e il suo tempo*, Todi, 1959, pp. 30–5.
78 Desbonnets and Vorreux, *Saint François*, see 'Joie', pp. 1514, 1537.
79 *De adventu*, 7.
80 *Ibid.*, 26.
81

Tria sunt necessaria ad salutem temporalem, cibus, somnus et iocus. Item iniunxit cuidam fratri melancholico ut biberet calicem plenum optimo vino pro poenitentia, et cum ebibisset, licet invitissime, dixit ei: Frater carissime, si haberes frequenter talem poenitentiam, haberes utique meliorem conscientiam.

(*Ibid.*, 92)

82 Cf. I Magli, *Gli uomini della penitenza*, Milan, 1977, which rightly makes Francis 'un uomo della penitenza' and suggests the interesting expression 'una cultura penitenziale'. Likewise, Giovanni Miccoli describes the Franciscans as a 'gruppo de penitenti' ('La storia religioso', p. 734).
83 See M. D'Altri (ed.), *Il movimento francescano della penitenza nella società medioevale* (Secondo Convegno di studi francescani, Padua, 1979), Rome, 1980.
84 *La povertà del secolo XII e Francesco d'Assisi* (Atti del II Convegno internazionale della Società internazionale di studi francescani, Assisi, 1974), Assisi, 1975.
85 One may also refer to the works of Michel Mollat and his students.
86 Fr. Willibrord, *Le Message spirituel de saint François d'Assise dans ses écrits*, Blois, 1960, see 'Humilité', pp. 238–40.
87 Excellent comments by Miccoli, 'La storia religiosa', p. 757.
88 E. Longpré, in the article 'Frères Mineurs' in the *Dictionnaire de spiritualité*, V, 1964, p. 1290, lists all the passages in the writings of Saint Francis and of his biographers where the idea is expressed that humility or inner poverty implies the disapproval of any public office (of any power).
89 Same attitude in Jacopone da Todi. Arsenio Frugoni could write, 'Jacopone hated the body with all his might' (Convegno di storia della spiritualità medievale, Todi, 1959, p. 86).
90 References may be found in *La Prière au Moyen Âge (Littérature et civilisation)*, *Senefiance*, 10, Aix-en-Provence and Paris, 1981.
91 A. Vauchez, *La Sainteté en Occident aux derniers siècles du Moyen Âge d'après les procès de canonisation et les documents hagiographiques*, Rome, 1981,

notably 'Les ordres mendiants et la sainteté locale', pp. 243–55, and 'La sainteté des ordres mendiants', pp. 388–409.

92

> Non contenti narrare solum miracula, quae sanctitatem non faciunt sed ostendunt, sed etiam sanctae conversationis eius insignia et pii beneplaciti voluntatem ostendere cupientes, ad laudem et gloriam summi Dei et dicti patris sanctissimi, atque aedificationem volentium eius vestigia imitari.
>
> (*Legenda trium sociorum*, ed. Desbonnets and Vorreux, *Saint François d'Assise* p. 89)

93 See J. Le Goff, 'Les rêves dans la culture et la psychologie collective de l'Occident médiéval', *Scolies*, I, 1971, pp. 123–30, also in *Pour un autre Moyen Âge*, pp. 299–306.

94 G. Zen and G. Sauro, *I sogni di san Francesco d'Assisi*, Asolo, 1975.

95 Desbonnets and Vorreux, *Saint François d'Assise*, see 'Vision', 1551 (long list).

96 See F. Cardini, 'San Francesco e il sogno delle armi'.

97 Cf. *Sancti Antonii de Padua Vitae due*, ed. L. Kerval, 1904.

98 A. Goddu, 'The Failure of Exorcism', *Miscellanea Mediaevalia*, 12/2: *Soziale Ordnungen im Selbsverstandnis des Mittelalters*, Berlin, 1980, pp. 540–57.

99 Desbonnets and Vorreux, *Saint François d'Asssise*, see 'Démon', p. 1531.

100 A. Stussi, 'Un serventese contro i frati tra ricette mediche del secolo XIII', in *L'Italia dialettale*, 30, 1967, p. 148, cited by Miccoli, 'La storia religiosa', p. 767.

101 On the Mendicants as disseminators of traditional ideas and as preachers of resignation under the guise of hostility towards the rich and towards established society, see Miccoli, 'La storia religiosa', pp. 798–9 and 803–6.

❖ ❖

BIBLIOGRAPHY

Editions and studies of works of Saint Francis

L. F. Benedetto, *Il Cantico di frate Sole*, Florence, 1950.

G. Cambell, 'Les écrits de saint François d'Assise devant la critique', *Franziskanische Studien*, 36, 1954.

V. Facchinetti and G. Cambell, *Gli scritti di san Francesco d'Assisi*, Milan, 1954, 1962 [5].

A. Quaglia, *Origini e sviluppi della regola francescana*, Naples, 1928.

—— *L'originalità della regola francescana*, Sassoferrato, 1943.

G. Sabatelli, 'Studi recenti sul Cantico di frate Sole', *Archivum franciscanum historicum*, 51, 1958.

Fr Willibrord, *Le Message spirituel de saint François d'Assise dans ses écrits*, Blois, 1960.

Biographical sources and studies of the sources

M. Bihl, *Sacrum Commercium S. F. cum domina Paupertate*, Quaracchi, 1929.

B. Bughetti and R. Pratesi, *I fioretti di san Francesco*, Florence, 1958.

E. Pistelli, *Le sacre nozze del beato francesco con Madonna povertà*, Foligno, 1926.

Modern biographies and general studies

U. Cosmo, *Con Madonna povertà* (Studi francescani), Bari, 1940.

P. Cuthbert, *Life of St. Francis of Assisi*, London, 1912, 1921 [2].

O. Englebert, *Vie de saint François d'Assise*, Paris, 1947, 1956 [2].

V. Facchinetti, *San Francesco d'Assisi nella storia, nella leggenda, nell'arte*, Milan, 1926.

BIBLIOGRAPHY

H. Felder, *Die Ideale des Hl. Franziskus von Assisi*, Paderborn, 1951 (new edn).

—— *Der Christusritter aus Assisi*, Zurich and Altstetten, 1941.

Gratien de Paris, *Histoire de la fondation et de l'évolution de l'ordre des frères Mineurs au XIIIe siècle*, Paris and Gembloux, 1928.

J. Jörgensen, *Den Hellige Franz af Assisi*, Copenhagen, 1907.

M. Niccoli, 'San Francesco d'Assisi', in *Enciclopedia italiana*, 1932.

P. Sabatier, *Vie de saint François d'Assise*, Paris, 1894, 1931.

—— *Études inédites sur saint François d'Assise*, Paris, 1932.

L. Salvatorelli, *Vita di san Francesco d'Assisi*, Bari, 1926.

—— 'Movimento francescano e gioachimismo. La storiografia francescana contemporanea', *X Congresso internazionale di scienze storiche, Relazione*, III (*Storia del Medioevo*), Rome, 1955.

Studies

L. Celluci, *Le leggende francescane de sec. XIII nel loro aspetto artistico*, Modena, 1929, 1957[2].

E. Delaruelle, 'L'influence de saint François d'Assise sur la piété populaire', *X Congresso internazionale di scienze storiche, Relazioni*, III (*Storia del Medioevo*), Rome, 1955.

V. Facchinetti, *Iconografia francescana*, Milan, 1924.

H. Focillon, *Saint François d'Assise et la peinture italienne au XIIIe et au XIVe siècle* (Moyen Âge: survivances et réveils), Montreal, 1945.

P. Francastel, 'L'art italien et le rôle personnel de saint François d'Assise', *Annales. E. S. C.*, 1956.

G. Kaftal, *St. Francis in Italian Painting*, London, 1950.

—— *Iconography of the Saints in Tuscan Painting*, Florence, 1952.

F. D. Klingender, 'St. Francis and the Birds of the Apocalypse', *Journal of the Warburg and Courtauld Institute*, XVI, 1953.

G. D. Ladner, 'Das älteste Bild des Hl. Franziskus von Assisi. Ein Beitrag zur mittelalterlichen Porträtikonographie', in *Mélanges Percy Ernst Schramm*, I, Wiesbaden, 1964.

M. Meiss, *Giotto and Assisi*, New York, 1960.

M. Meiss and L. Tintori, *The Painting of the Life of St. Francis of Assisi with Notes on the Arena Chapel*, New York, 1962.

R. Offner, 'Note on an unknown St. Francis in the Louvre', *Gazette des beaux-arts*, February 1962.

P. Sabatier, A. Masseron, H. Hauvette, H. Focillon, E. Gilson and E. Jordan, *L'Influence de saint François d'Assise sur la civilisation italienne*, Paris, 1926.

H. Thode, *Franz von Assisi und die Anfänge der Kunst des Renaissance in Italien*, 1889, 1926[3].

Franciscan landscapes

P. N. Cavanna, *L'Umbria francescana illustrata*, Perugia, 1910.

BIBLIOGRAPHY

A. Fortini, *Assisi nel Medio Evo*, Rome, 1940.

A. Frugoni, 'Subiaco francescano', *Bollettino dell'Instituto italiano per il Medio Evo*, 65 (1953).

J. Jörgensen, *Pèlerinages franciscains*, Paris, 1912.

Saint Francis and the religious history of the Middle Ages

E. Buonaiuti, *La prima Rinascita. Il profeta: Gioacchino da Fiore. Il missionario: Francesco di Assisi. Il cantore: Dante*, Milan, 1952.

M.-D. Chenu, 'L'expérience des Spirituels au XIIIe siècle', *Lumière et vie*, 10, 1953.

E. Benz, *Ecclesia Spiritualis. Kirchenidee und Geschichtstheologie der franziskanischen Reformation*, Stuttgart, 1934.

H. Grundmann, *Religiöse Bewegungen im Mittelalter*, Berlin, 1961 [2].

Bibliographical supplement
Selected works published from 1967 to 1999

Sources

François d'Assise, Écrits, Introduction, translation and notes by Th. Desbonnets, J. F. Goddet and Th. Matura, Paris, Le Cerf/Éditions franciscaines, 1981.

Saint François d'Assise. Documents, écrits et premières biographies, assembled and introduced by Th. Desbonnets and D. Vorreux, Paris, Éditions franciscaines, [1968], 1981 [2].

Studies

1968. A. Vauchez, 'Les stigmates de saint François et leurs détracteurs dans les derniers siècles du Moyen Âge', *Mélanges d'archéologie et d'histoire*, Rome, École française de Rome, vol. 80, pp. 595–625.

1981. R. Manselli, *Saint François d'Assise* (Italian original, 1980), Paris, Éditions franciscaines.

1983. Th. Desbonnets, *De l'intuition à l'institution. Les franciscains*, Paris, Éditions franciscaines.

1983. *Francesco d'Assisi nella storia*, vol. I, Convegno di studi, sec. XIII–XV, Rome, Instituto storico dei Cappucini.

1983. D. Flood, *Frère François et le mouvement franciscain*, Paris, Éditions ouvrières.

1984. A. Bartolilangeli, 'Le radici culturali della popolarità francescana', in *Il francescanismo e il teatro medievale* (colloquium of San Miniato, 1982), Castelfiorentino (Biblioteca della Miscellanea storica della Valdera, 6), pp. 41–58.

1988. Ch. Frugoni, *Francesco, un'altra storia*, Genoa, Marietti.

BIBLIOGRAPHY

1991. G. Miccoli, *Francesco d'Assisi. Realtà e memoria di un'esperienza cristiana*, Turin, Einaudi.

1991. G. G. Merlo, *Tra eremo e città. Studi su Francesco d'Assisi e sul francescanismo*, Assisi (Saggi, 2).

1991. G. G. Merlo, 'La storiografia francescana dal dopoguerra a oggi', *Studi storici*, pp. 287–307.

1993. Ch. Frugoni, *Francesco e l'invenzione delle stimmate. Una storia per immagini e parole fino a Giotto ed a Bonaventura*, Turin, Einaudi.

1994. W. Schenkluhn, *San Francesco in Assisi. Ecclesia specialis*, Milan.

1994. H. Feld, *Franziskus von Assisi und seine Bewegung*, Darmstadt, Wiss. Buchges.

1996. S. Dalarun, *La malavventura di Francesco d'Assisi. Per un uso storico delle legende francescane*, Milan (Fonti e richerche, 10).

1996. Th. Matura, *François d'Assise, 'auteur spirituel'*, Paris, Éditions du Cerf.

1997. J. Dalarun, *François d'Assise, un passage. Femme et fémininité dans les écrits et les légendes franciscaines*, Arles (original Italian, 1994).

1997. F. Accrocca, *Francesco e le sue immagini, Momenti della evoluzione della coscienza storica dei frati minori (sec. XIII–XVI)*, Padua, Centro di studi antoniani, 27.

1997. *Francesco d'Assisi e il primo secolo di storia francescana*, Turin (Biblioteca Einaudi, 1).

1998. G. Bessière and H. Vulliez, *Frère François. Le saint d'Assise*, Paris, Gallimard.

1998. T. Buongiorno and Ch. Frugoni, *Storia di Francesco. Il santo che sapeva ridere*, Rome and Bari, Laterza.

1998. Chiara Frugoni, *Francis of Assisi: A Life*, trans. from the Italian, New York.

1999. J. Dalarun, *François d'Assise ou le pouvoir en question. Principes et modalités du gouvernement dans l'ordre des Frères mineurs*, Paris and Brussels, DeBoeck Université.

Music

O. Messiaen, *Saint François d'Assise: scènes franciscaines*, opera created in Paris in 1983.

Cinema

R. Rossellini, *The Flower of St Francis*, Italian film, 1950.

CD

François d'Assise, by Jacques Le Goff, Paris, Gallimard, 1998.